Restaurants Also Serve Food

Restaurants Also Serve Food

Peter Backman

political animal
PRESS

Political Animal Press
www.politicalanimalpress.com

Distributed by the University of Toronto Press
www.utpdistribution.com
University of Toronto Press
5201 Dufferin Street
Toronto, Ontario, Canada
M3H 5T8

Cataloguing data available from Library and Archives Canada

ISBN 978-1895131-36-9 (paperback)
ISBN 978-1895131-37-6 (eBook)

Cover design by Islam Farid.

Contents

An Introduction – What you can expect from this book

This book is for you if you sell successfully to multiple retailers like Tesco or Waitrose or Aldi, but make a real hash of selling to foodservice operators – to restaurants, pubs, hotels, schools, contract caterers and all the rest. After all, they buy food don't they? Yes they do but there's a big difference. Multiple retailers buy food and then sell food; foodservice operators buy food and then sell an experience. For them, food is a much smaller part of their success. This book is about why this matters. So let's find out.

Just imagine you are flying over the Alps in your air-conditioned plane. It is cloudy down below – in fact all you can see are the peaks of mountains that have punched their way through the clouds. You try to guess what it looks like beneath the clouds. But the peaks you can see are no guide to the valleys below. They won't tell you about the raging torrents and the gentle grasslands; the cities and small towns; the wooded valleys and the impenetrable forests; the people and the farms.

So it is with the restaurant business. The mountain peaks you can see are like data we can find on the eating-out market. While this information is available and may be accurate, it is not necessarily very helpful in identifying what's happening.

This book is intended to provide ground rules on the wider view below. It's not a 'How To' book. It offers something altogether different – an explanation of the currents and flows of the foodservice sector and its supply chain, and insights into how the various sectors interact. With these insights you, the reader, will be better able to make the decisions that matter to you.

When you get into the book, you may be asking yourself after a few pages, 'Why all this emphasis on the retailing market?' The answer is that the media, and many suppliers, create a single entity that combines foodservice (eating out in restaurants, at work, in hotels and more) and food retailing (through grocers, supermarkets, independent food stores and the like). After all, they both provide food, don't they? Well, yes. But foodservice is perhaps more accurately called 'serviced food', a term referring to all meals provided outside the home. It's an ugly phrase, not easy to understand, which is why the Americans invented the word 'foodservice' twenty years ago or so. That term captures the spirit, if not the complete picture, of this diverse sector.

Food retailing is different as we shall see. And that's why suppliers who have a foot in both retail and foodservice camps need to be fully informed about their differences.

I have been researching the foodservice market for over thirty years. And I have been advising suppliers for almost all of that time. Although there are many people in the foodservice supply chain who know much – and in their chosen spheres they know more than me – the foodservice market in its totality, including its supply chain, suffers from a lack of knowledge and consequently suppliers have too many unreal expectations of what they can expect from foodservice, and how to make progress in the sector.

Consequently, investment gets skewed and commitments get pulled prematurely. As a result, what is needed is clear analysis and, as I argue throughout this book, accurate information about what foodservice actually is and, given its nature, what results can be expected from it.

Over the years, I have attended network sessions, conferences, client meetings, and presentations without number. I have read articles, academic papers, magazines, blogs, and tweets. I have been involved in phone calls and briefing sessions beyond counting. I have spoken to journalists, consultants, TV broadcasters, and academics. Each experience and each contact has contributed something to the store of my knowledge. And the names of the people I have worked with over the years, as colleagues, clients, and competitors are far too many to mention, but I have learned something from each of them. Individually I have learned small things – collectively I have learned much; my thanks go to everyone I have learned from.

And in the pages that follow I will be sharing with you what I have learned.

The more you know about the foodservice market, the more likely you are to make a success of selling to it. This book will increase your knowledge significantly.

Bright New Dawn

To find out where I am leading you, let's start at the very beginning and take a short journey.

You are the CEO of a big-name manufacturer or you are the Managing Director of a small business, perhaps family owned or the national subsidiary of an international player. Maybe the world is your oyster – you have the option to supply the retail sector or foodservice, and you are not sure which path to tread. Or perhaps you have 'strategy' somewhere in your job description or you hold an important sales or marketing role. Your products are food or drink or the household goods that consumers want every day or every week – toiletries, cleaning products, or disposables.

You inhabit a world of order and structure. Sure, things go wrong. Maybe an unexpected tax that impacts your products or the markets you serve is imposed by the government of the day. Or there's a food scare that involves your company in some way. Or a competitor emerges unexpectedly. And things can happen at a less significant, but no less troublesome, level too. A trusted colleague decides to leave for pastures new; there's a fire in an important part of your production or distribution chain. And then there are the day-to-day troubles, issues, and small crises. But in the end, you are paid to handle these things. And that's made easier by the order in your world.

Just walk down to the production line. There's procedure here amid the rattling, murmuring, clattering, and chinking; unformed materials are transformed by machines and people into product. It is heated, cooled, cut, sliced, mixed, sorted; it is measured, marshalled, packed, and offloaded. It is put into boxes. Boxes are placed in cases. Cases are packed on pallets. Pallets are wrapped in plastic; they are stacked. Before not too long – quickly, because storing stuff costs money – the pallets are loaded onto lorries, and the lorries take their loads to a retailer's giant distribution centre at a road hub conveniently located for the towns and cities the retailer serves. The lorry disgorges its load via fork lifts, and it is stacked on shelves. And it is at about this point that your responsibilities end and become the retailer's.

Now, at their end, computerised orders instruct a small team (a large team costs a lot of money – and computers make massive efficiency gains here) to pick pallets. With the minimum time between delivery and despatch they are unloaded. Some pallets are broken down (undoing the careful building up work that you did in your factory) and their contents repackaged into metal cages. Pallets and cages are placed in computer ordained, carefully structured locations ready for loading onto monster 40-tonne trucks.

Pallets and cages are loaded and driven to the retailer's supermarkets. Just in time. They are taken into a storage area – a small area – because goods won't remain here long, if at all. Or they are taken from the truck straight into the supermarket.

And 'product', yours and many others, is stored in neat, pre-ordered rows on the shelves and gondola ends and at the checkout. The ordering of the products is driven by experience, often encoded in algorithms held in some-one's computer that maximise sales of the most profit-able items and allow maximum choice for the customer. Choice is important – not only to the costumer who may want something unusual – but also to the retailer who wants to be able to allow consumers to compare prices and offers before deciding what to buy.

This is where the customer's responsibilities begin. Eagerly pushing trolleys or carrying baskets, customers mull over, argue about, and chose from the multiplicity of offers on the shelves. They take them to the checkout where maybe there's a word or two with the assistant at the till but not, of course, if the customer uses the self-service checkout line where she is ordered what to do by a disembodied, computer-driven voice – and then off to the car with the groceries to be piled into the boot and driven home.

All of this is an organised system with solid under-pinnings of structures, computers, efficiency gains (small and large), and planning. It responds to the big shifts – changes in society, food purchasing moving to online delivery, developments in the ways that consumers view food, their requirements for new ways of cooking and serving food, and much more. And the system also reacts to immediate changes brought about by ordinary events, such as late deliveries because of traffic problems, or longer term, unforeseen changes that occur, say in patterns of consumer demand because of a rapid change in the weather or England unexpectedly winning a game in the World Cup.

Billions of items of information drive your view of your world. You receive up-to-date information about the performance of your products throughout the system. From EPOS data to consumer-generated data, all aggregated, sorted, analysed, and interpreted, perhaps by Artificial Intelligence algorithms, and if not, then interpreted by your sales or marketing colleagues. A flood of data that can be interpreted in a multitude of ways. Sliced and diced by product and category, by retailer and location, by time of day and day of the week, whether the product is on offer, or your competitor's product is on offer. Today sales are good, reversing two days of decline – that's a relief, but why did it happen in the first place?

And after a while you notice that sales are plateauing. You start to activate plans you've already spent some time developing. Or the data you have access to shows where there are gaps and opportunities that you can exploit straightaway. Maybe there's a product extension to hand, or you have devised a nifty way to develop your range that makes it even more appealing to customers and consumers, or you have a pricing initiative (already agreed with the retailer). Your plans are put into practice, and sales start to rise again.

There is order here, and planning. And your colleagues, who have grown up commercially by serving multiple retailers, by and large share your knowledge and view of the retail world. Communication with them is easy because you have common experiences, thoughts, and understanding of what works and why (and what doesn't work and why). You have the multiple retailers sewn up. Actually they have you sewn up too, but at least you know where you stand with them all – and there are only a handful to measure, monitor, sell to, and work with.

After a while you are looking for new fields to conquer. Things are going so well that it makes sense to look at new opportunities. Or maybe things aren't going so well: a retailer has cancelled a long-term relationship or sales are in decline because of a change in consumer preferences or a new competitor has emerged. Or maybe, because of your success, you have decided to invest in new production and warehousing facilities, and while your multiple supermarket customers will take quite a lot of the output, you still need to sell more to make the investment viable.

You look around and pretty soon your eyes alight on the foodservice sector which is growing and which uses your products. Perhaps you currently have a negligible presence here and see great opportunities to add to your sales prospects and pipeline. That's where you're going to place your efforts – or at least some of them.

No. Stop. Think. And don't cross that particular road until you have looked both ways.

●

I'm a successful supplier to retailers. How can I be a successful supplier to foodservice too? *Watch out! Being a successful retail supplier will not help you to be a successful foodservice supplier. You have the systems and mind set honed to the needs of retail – and these are out of sync with the needs of foodservice. Solution? Separate the two.*

Looking both ways.
It's all about food. Isn't it?

It's lunchtime and you are entertaining at The Wolsey in London's Piccadilly. You and your guest are greeted at the door, and after a quick discussion with the welcomer, you are shown to your table. A menu is placed in front of you, and you start talking to your guest. After a while a server walks up bringing some bread and olive oil, and she asks if you're ready to order drinks. Not long after, you signal that you are ready to order. And shortly your starters are delivered. You talk about business with your guest and the main course arrives. More discussion, maybe turning lightly towards forthcoming holidays. Then it's time for your dessert, and the conversation veers back to the business topic that you're there to discuss. With the coffee, you reach agreement. You chat inconsequentially, perhaps joshing about how well your county's cricket team is doing compared with his. You pay and leave.

At the same hour, your daughter, who is working as in intern with a City firm, is out for lunch with a couple of chums. She doesn't have much time so they pop into a nearby Prêt a Manger. They chose their food from the wide range sitting on the shelves. While queuing to pay, the three of them talk about this and that. They pay and take a seat by the window. They eat and talk. Soon they're finished. They put on their coats and walk out.

Meanwhile your youngest child is at school waiting patiently to be served lunch. He talks animatedly to his mates about whatever it is teenagers talk about and, choosing their dish, they are served by the chatty dinner lady behind the service counter. They pick up their trays and make their way to their table – always the same one where they spend a pleasant twenty minutes talking, arguing, and comparing notes. Clearing up their plates, trays, and cutlery, they place them on the trolley and saunter out into the sunshine.

What ties all these experiences together? Eating obviously – and therefore food and drink are an important part. But there is also anticipation of the food to come, interaction with people who wish to make the experience pleasurable, and talking to friends or colleagues. Thus, in essence, it's about taking time out from everyday activities in a relaxing setting.

While you are just finishing your meal at The Wolsey, your partner is sitting in front of the computer and punches in the username and password that provides access to the Ocado online supermarket website. Helpful computer- generated suggestions based on past experience appear on the screen, accompanied by price comparisons, providing a simple and efficient process by which to make decisions. Several hours later, maybe next day, the van arrives, the delivery is completed, and perhaps a word or two exchanged with the delivery driver.

Meanwhile, your third child is out doing some shopping for essentials of the moment. Walking into the shop, he goes up to the cabinet and selects the soft drink that is the object of his desire, and while on his way out, he buys a couple of items that catch his eye. Walking into the self-service checkout area, he is assailed by electronic voices informing him what to do, where to place his goods, asking whether he has a bag, how much his purchases cost, directing him what to do next. Soon it's his turn to be fed through this system. He makes a mistake, and an assistant is called over, silently he makes some apparently random entries into the key pad, and order is restored. Your son pays. And he walks out.

Now, let's consider the differences you and your family would have experienced in these activities – eating out on the one hand and ordering or buying food on the other. Both are about getting food, of course. But, when eating out, personal interaction as you are being served is an important and a significantly enjoyable part of the experience; in ordering or buying food in a shop, personal interaction is either non-existent or very limited. This is a vital difference that I advise you strongly to consider as you make your plans. Foodservice is not only about food – it's also about service. And of the two, service is the more important. And when you add into the mix the level of social interaction with family or friends, and the anticipation and enjoyment, it's clear that eating out is a three-legged activity and depends on food, service, and something about human conviviality that we can characterise as experience.

Buying food from a shop, on the other hand, is about efficiency and transactions. In a shop, you've spent money and not spoken a word to anyone. Your main interaction with the shop has been reading what's on the packet, on the shelf, or in the freezer cabinet. Efficient – probably; heart-warming – no.

You've eaten in a restaurant, you've spent time eating and chatting. Then it's time to leave – you ask for the bill and pay. Perhaps you leave a tip and the waiter smiles. Efficient – not very; heart-warming yes.

These descriptions are somewhat embellished simply to make a point. Not all food-buying experiences, even in a supermarket, are as soulless as I've described. Supermarkets nowadays have deli counters and bakery sections manned by people in fetching uniforms, gingham aprons, rakish head coverings – and, of course, rubber gloves. But the promise of special, knowledgeable service that these accoutrements, based on long-ago food shopping, imply is not really available. Most products are pre-packed and ready to purchase with the minimum of interaction between server and shopper. 'Give me one of those and one of those please', and they're off

But, I can hear you say, of course this picture of retailing may be true of food retailing, but surely it's not so true about selling other products – clothes, for instance, or hardware. But I would respond that many sectors where relationships once were important in the purchase decision – books for example, or clothes – used to involve, perhaps even relied on, advice and comment from the person behind the counter. Nowadays purchases of items like these are dependent on IT; they are transactional and lacking in soul. Just like buying food from a shop in fact. Purchasing in so many sectors has radically changed. But not in the foodservice sector!

So I'll repeat my main point but in a slightly different way: retail is all about efficiency; eating out is all about making you feel good. And this fundamental difference means that you, as a supplier, must adjust your approach to the foodservice sector. You have to recognise its basic role as a service provider is one that requires such soft skills as courtesy, friendliness, respect, attentiveness, all of which make customers feel welcome.

Here is what I mean. Not long ago, I was briefly introduced to André Mannini, the great Ops Director of the highly successful M Restaurant in London. Later, he sent me an email saying 'Do let me know if you are around one of our venues in the future – I would love to say hi and buy you a drink!' Can you imagine the Ops Director of a multiple retailer sending you an email saying he'd love to say hi and buy you a trolleyful of groceries?

But please don't assume that commercial success in the foodservice sector is simple – and that all you have to do is apply some of those soft skills, tickle some tummies, and they'll roll over and snaffle the apple from your outstretched hand. Far from it – very far from it.

This is where we get to the nub of my argument, and if you take nothing else away from this book, it's what I'd like you to remember: it is vitally important to recognise that the agenda of people who work in the foodservice business is different from the retailer's agenda.

As someone who is supplying (or would like to supply) the people and businesses in foodservice, your challenge is how you can meet them on their terms and not on the terms you have used successfully in selling to people and businesses in the retail space who want order and structure and predicted outcomes in terms of rate of sale and ROI (return on investment) and a host of other KPIs (key performance indicators).

The decisions made in the foodservice sector that lead up to the purchase of whatever it is you want to supply – food or beverage, equipment or paper cups, furniture or lighting – will have been based on whether your product provides or enhances a welcoming, hospitable environment. You'll have to work hard to understand what your customer – and the market you're addressing today – wants, and you'll have had to do lots of groundwork.

But don't forget that when it comes to the actual purchase decision, you'll find that self-interest kicks in. The owner of a café or the tenant of a pub, the chef at a small care home, or the manager of a B&B will be doing their shopping at the cash and carry with a clear idea in their mind of what they want and how much they're prepared to pay. They'll compare and examine in some detail, and only then will they decide. Your product, which you've worked so hard to get on the shelf, will fail unless your offer – price, quality, promise, packaging, and the rest – are right and bear comparison with other products. Just like the retail customer in fact!

At the other end of the size spectrum, the buyer at a contract caterer handling a food budget in the hundreds of millions of pounds has enormous buying power to wield, and although there aren't that many of them, plenty of companies do spend tens of millions of pounds. People in these businesses will be hard to convince, and price will have a significant role to play – but it's not the only factor at play. For example, if you know more about the market than your competitors, you will be seen as representing a company that adds value to the buyer's role.

In between the café proprietor and the contract catering buyer are a whole plethora of hard-nosed buyers who will be looking for a deal that will add to their employing company's net earnings or EBITDA.

If foodservice were a person what it would look like? No – this isn't a question taken out of some psychology textbook or a text book on how to sell into different markets. There is a purpose behind the question – and it's probably not what you think.

So, if foodservice were a person what characteristics would you notice? I have asked lots of people this question, and from their comments I've extracted the key words. Here they are:

Hospitable   Helpful
Loyal   Entrepreneurial
Flamboyant   Interesting
Fun   Friendly
Engaging   Market trader
Fragmented   Full of new ideas
Unpredictable   Risk-taker
Poor planner   Confused
Informal   Unclear

Many of these descriptors suggest a hospitable persona – and, of course, that's totally understandable because serving food is all about hospitality.

Now think about retailing. If retailing were a person what would its characteristics be? I've asked this question too, and here are the adjectives associated with the answers:

Structured	Armed
Systematic	Loaded
Data-driven	Performance-driven
Informed	Army Major
Directed	Formulaic
Assertive	Agile
Strategic	New
Risk-taker	Results-driven
Diverse	Powerful

Now both of these activities – foodservice and retail – are concerned with serving food. But the way in which they carry it out is very different.

Retail is all about efficiency, systems, just in time, driving down costs, investing in hubs, and other activities directed at squeezing every penny of profit out of the system. To drive this machine requires operators with the required skills – and the retail business quite rightly attracts people who can drive efficiency, squeeze out costs, think strategically.

In turn, the retail system that they drive, calls upon suppliers that have the same attributes. The retail sector and its supply chain are aligned on the 'knowing' plane, and manufacturers that successfully supply the retail sector have the 'knowing' approach that works in retail.

Now take foodservice, where its operators are working in a craft environment, no two days are the same, no two customers are alike, and where flexibility, customer smiles, and appreciation are key metrics. The person who thrives in such an environment has personality traits that match these requirements. Typically, they are 'people people' and occupy the 'feeling' space.

And as you become acquainted with their supply chain, you'll find the people with those same sorts of attributes are the successful suppliers. Food manufacturers that succeed in foodservice are suppliers with a pronounced 'feeling' aspect to their relationships.

But food manufacturers – especially large suppliers – supply both foodservice and retail. And that's where foodservice 'feeling' and retail 'knowing' meet.

Although the foodservice sector is populated by people whose business success is built around personal relationships, and whose one-word characteristic is hospitable, the interface between your company and the foodservice operator that really counts – the sale – is hard-nosed and is where self-interest plays a great part in the decision.

And I haven't even mentioned the large operators that require a standardised product and buy a small, limited range. The fast-food giants – in burger, coffee, pizza, that sort of thing – work closely with their suppliers to create bespoke products that will be bought in large quantities, that must meet detailed and challenging standards, day in and day out, without deviating from the agreed specifications. And all of this must be supplied at a price that is as low as possible. But not so low that it will bankrupt you, the supplier, because it makes no sense for your fast-food customer to devote energy to creating products with you and agreeing on terms, only to see you fall over.

Here, the purchase decision is also going to be hard-nosed, but the factors leading up to it will be permeated with the welcoming gene.

Nor have I talked about the biggest buyers of all – the wholesalers (and the buyers at cash and carries). These are the closest you'll get in foodservice to a retailer. They handle a wide range – tens of thousands of items for sale (SKUs) – they'll have lots of customers, again tens of thousands (but not the tens of millions that shop at your retail customers' outlets). The buyers at the wholesalers are cut from a similar cloth as the buyers you meet in the retail sector. In fact, they may be the same people who have job-shifted from retailing to wholesaling. But when you deal with them, you should always remember that they are in the business of dealing with foodservice operators and understand what kind of personality fits with their customers, i.e. welcoming and hospitable.

So just remember that the buyer to whom you sell performs a hard-nosed, transactional function, but lives in a forest where hospitality rules.

Before we leave this chaper, I should note that not every foodservice operation emphasises human relations. There are, inevitably, wide deviations in such a large complex sector, one that has been going strong for hundreds of years. For example, customer experiences in some foodservice environments are quite close to their retail experiences. Take food-to-go. The customer walks in, selects a product from a chilled cabinet. Walks over to the serving station. Pays and leaves – or pays and eats in.

This raises a concept that has now entered the food-service sector, called 'blurring'. It recognises that some of the differences between retail and foodservice are being eliminated, or at least rubbed over.

That certainly occurs in some sectors. I just mentioned food-to-go, which is probably the most obvious example of blurring or the erosions of the line between foodservice and retail.

All I have to say on this to you as a potential practitioner in selling to these two sectors is: be aware of blurring. Indeed, on some occasions you would be advised to put on your retail cap when talking to foodservice.

So to summarise, crucial to understanding how to approach the foodservice sector is your recognition of the fundamental differences between foodservice and food retail, how these differences impact on ways you should interact with the foodservice sector, and what this means for your business.

In a nutshell: foodservice is not about food – it's about other things. What are these other things, and how do you incorporate them into your way of dealing with the foodservice sector? That's a question that we'll turn to now.

●

Words are important. *The word foodservice has 11 letters and only one third of them are 'food'; two thirds are 'service'. So it is with the eating-out experience – food is a third of the experience, service is two thirds.*

What's in a name?

In this chapter you will indeed find out what's in a name. Should you use the term 'foodservice'? Why or why not?

So let's explore. The denizens of the market that you refer to as 'foodservice' will look at you in bemusement if you say they are involved in foodservice. Someone who runs a restaurant will think of himself as a restaurateur (incidentally, not a restauranteur – the 'n' is not part of the job), and if she is a technocratic manager, she will probably refer to herself as a restaurant operator. A publican is just that, a publican whether he's pulling a pint or preparing a pie. Calling him a foodservice operator will strike him as bizarre.

Similarly, the person in charge of the food in a hotel will be known as an F&B, i.e. a food and beverage, manager. Or maybe if she manages just the restaurant, she will think of herself as a restaurateur or as a restaurant manager. The person responsible for providing food to children five days a week at a school will be a school meals organiser, and the lady who prepares the food, and dishes it out is probably called a dinner lady.

And the same goes for hamburger operators, hospital kitchen managers, and even the people who provide food in prisons. Dinner lady, restaurateur, F&B manger, school meals organiser, and all the rest. But not a mention of foodservice.

It's just you and your colleagues and your competitors, people who happily supply them with food or equipment or janitorial supplies or some of the thousands of other products that they buy, who refers to them as 'foodservice'.

Does it matter? Well, here are a few considerations.

It matters because when you talk to these people you should talk to them as they think of themselves. It's true that in all my years being involved in the sector I can't think of a single occasion when someone has been upset or disconcerted by being referred to as being in 'foodservice', but it's just sensible to name them according to the profession they see themselves in.

And here's another reason. By using the generic term 'foodservice', you will tend to brush away the complexity of the market with all its fine-grained distinctions between F&B manager and restaurateur, between publican and dinner lady. This doesn't matter to the people you are talking to. But it matters hugely to you if it means that you blur these distinctions in your own mind. You won't be alive to the differences and won't take them into account when you make decisions about the sector.

Many of the names we currently use in the foodservice sector have a historical origin that reminds us of their function. For example, the word 'restaurant' is derived from the French verb 'restaurer', meaning 'to restore'.

You went to a restaurant to be emotionally, spiritually, healthily restored, to have your need for food and comfort satisfied. Restaurants are still there to restore the guest. In other words, hospitality is at the heart of what a restaurant offers.

The word 'pub' picks up this theme too. It is of course, a shortened form of the phrase 'public house' and a house, a home, is where you feel comfortable and where you look after guests hospitably by making them feel welcome and addressing their needs as best you can. A public house originally was actually an ordinary house that was open to anyone to supply them with alcohol, spirits like gin, and beer and wine. But the concept of welcoming, again of being hospitable, runs through the veins of every pub. The Victorians talked about 'mine host' – the person who ran the pub was a host to his guests, his customers.

And the word 'host' comes from hospitality, just as the word 'hotel' does. Even 'hospital' comes from hospitality, as a hospital is a place where the concept of restoring the body was, and still is, the driving force.

What all this tells us, is that the idea of welcoming, of being hospitable, has infused the way we talk about the sector that we now call by its utilitarian name of 'foodservice'. Even 'service' implies (or it certainly should imply) doing what is possible to 'repair' the guest and to make him or her somehow whole again. In outmoded English, guests were said to 'repair' to their meal – and there was clearly a reason for using the word.

So, make a solemn promise not to use the term 'food-service' in front of those people who work in the industry – if you can!

Having said that no-one in the sector you call 'food-service' refers to themselves in that way, I must note an exception. People who are involved in outsourced catering used to be called caterers, or contract caterers – and many still do use that terminology. But nowadays they are just as likely to refer to their sector of the market as food service. But note that this term is two words – and there is a reason. It is because it is coupled with facilities management in the phrase 'food and facilities management service'. So what's all this about?

Contract caterers provide meals in places which are run by people whose core business is not providing food – they may be providing financial services or caring for patients in a hospital or manufacturing motor cars or writing software. Rather than trying to do all things, they contract out things that are not central to their way of working such as, and especially in the context of this book, the provision of meals in their cafeterias or dining rooms or staff restaurants. And they can and do contract out their other non-core activities, such as cleaning or their security services or their print room or their reception desk, and many more. Activities such as these are grouped together under the heading of 'facilities management', and the companies that provide the canteen services also provide facilities management services.

As a result providers of these services increasingly nowadays call themselves 'food service' or 'food and facilities management services'. So it is acceptable to address these people as Mr. Food Service – but please remember to use two words!

So far, we have talked about foodservice (and also food service in two words) but you may, because many people do, refer to a market that is called Away From Home or Out of Home or even by acronyms like AFH and OOH. I can tell you straight away that nobody but you and other suppliers like you refers to the sector like this. Certainly, nobody active in any sector that we've just talked about refers to themselves in these ways.

So please do not use the word 'foodservice' or the phrases 'away from home' or 'out of home' to any coffee shop operator or leisure site manager or restaurateur or publican or anyone else like them. These terms won't mean anything to them. They reflect your world where they are all used to distinguish this market from the market that you call 'retail'.

In other words, you have a bilateral view which says the world is either 'Retail' or 'Everything else'. Retail sells food for people to eat at home – or nearly at home – and Foodservice or Away from Home or Out of Home or worse, OOH – is everything else. This attitude underestimates this eating-out market, which represents nearly 30% of everything we Brits spend on food. It also ignores the complexity of the market.

So what's in a name? An awful lot is the answer, especially when you look at the many different sectors of the eating-out market, each with its own unique customer demographics, trading styles, food offers, pricing, terminology – the list of differences goes on and on.

And also remember that the use of portmanteau words – like foodservice or OOH – may cause complications as the person you are talking to and selling to won't relate to this terminology. So avoid using it in public!

But, and whisper it very quietly, it's OK to use it between ourselves – just because it's us, and we know what we are referring to when we use the term foodservice. So that's what I'll be doing throughout the rest of this book.

What happens when you call on Foodservice? *When you knock on the door and you call Foodservice – nobody is in.*

'Magic'. Is the brand king?

Do you own a brand – or a stable of brands – that you nourish and scrub to ensure that its positioning is constant and understood? And do you place great value on your brand?

Well, you need to understand how people in the food-service sector view brands. It's not straightforward – indeed it's very nuanced – and in this chapter, we'll take a look at some of these distinctions.

First let's look at the split between front of house and back of house. Front of house is the customer-facing part of the operation; it's what the customer sees – and back of house is all the other bits, especially, for our purposes, the kitchen.

Now consider a restaurant and coffee shop – put them side by side. One works its magic behind the scenes, and the other is straightforward and visible to the customer. The meal served to you in a restaurant is made up from a whole larder full of component foods, all usually prepared out of sight. Restaurateurs – whether they run high-end, Michelin-starred operations or mid-market, casual dining brands or almost any other kind of restaurant – want their customers to experience some magic when food is put in front of them.

And sometimes the magic extends to where the ingredients come from. But not always! For example, in some restaurants or hotels – where the provenance is important and the restaurateur or the hotelier believes it is worth making an effort to obtain certain special products – the source of meat, the produce, the fish may be described with loving care. And in others, these same ingredients are just regarded as generic products, albeit of high or at least adequate quality, safe, and desirable to eat.

But turning back to the magic: for most restaurants and other operators, the brands of their products are never revealed to the customer – whether it's the mayonnaise, the custard, or the soup – the brand is not for the customer to know. And if the customer doesn't know, he or she will assume that it's made in the kitchen (even if it isn't). That's a part of the magic in action.

But, there's another complication. In some restaurants, the customer is offered additional options on the table top – tomato ketchup, for example, or sugar or mustard. And in some of those restaurants, the brand they use is worth promoting, especially when it is consistent with the positioning of the outlet. A workman-style table-top product, for example, can be a helpful and credible complement to a workman-style café or workplace. By the same token, the breakfast room in an expensive hotel can openly present a branded jar of an upmarket jam to its customers when the brand values of the hotel and the jam coincide.

So there are opportunities for your brand, in some instances, in some restaurants – but not in most instances, in most restaurants.

In a coffee shop, on the other hand, the magic still exists but is much more readily complemented with brands – of confectionery and biscuits for example. Here the brand can be much more heroic.

And, as a general rule, for products that consumers would know and that must be bought in, but not made, by the operator, such as soft drinks or wine or beer or tea or even jam or mustard (and these are only some examples), brands are important. And they are important in the eating-out space for the same reason they are important in retail shops. They provide assurance about the quality, not just of the particular venue, but also of the kind of service on offer.

But, and it's really worth noting, the brand in a foodservice outlet may be a special brand – perhaps with up-market aspirations – that the customer may not have access to through normal retail channels. The magic continues.

So, having travelled this far, what have we learned? Foodservice operators want to create magic for their customers – and this applies across the spectrum from run-of-the-mill food-to-go operations to Michelin five-starred restaurants. Brands may be used more freely in some places than in others, but where they are used, they often impart their own magic.

And here's the killer: everyday brands that are to be found freely available in retail outlets are not magic because, and please note this, the customer can see them – and use them – in their own kitchens. The price of a brand that is available in the retail sector is (or may be) known to the customer who may be eating out. And a mismatch in pricing can remove the magic and, even damage consumer perceptions of the brand or the operator or both.

And here I'll add the point that sometimes the food-service brand returns the compliment. Some restaurant chains use the magic of their brand to promote products made for the retailer – whether it's a pizza or piri-piri sauce. Whether this adds to or subtracts from the allure of the magic of the restaurant brand is a moot point.

This has just been a gentle spin around front of house; there is much more to this, but we are running out of space and we have to turn to the back-of-house operation, those bits that aren't front of house, especially the kitchen. Also under this heading I'd include central kitchens (or commissaries) where food is made for a number of remote operations.

Here a useful split to keep in mind is between operations where decisions are made in the kitchen – these are generally, but certainly not exclusively, independent outlets – and those where decision making takes place up and down a whole chain, right up to the head office, and where the kitchen may not even be involved. These are almost exclusively group operators.

So, whenever you look at when, if, and how to use a brand front and centre when selling into the back-of-house function, consider this distinction between independent or group operators.

And independent operators can be further split into those where the decision maker is experienced and comfortable in making decisions about what food to purchase, and those where there is a relative lack of experience about these matters.

So, we have three types of businesses to consider: independent operations where lack of experience (or confidence) is the norm, independent operations where there is plenty of experience, and group operations. And the branded foods and any other products you supply have different roles to play in each type of business.

The inexperienced kitchen has its own areas of experience, buying the main products – meat, fish, poultry, produce – and perhaps some other categories as well – cheese, sauces, and soup. But that leaves lots of other products where the person making the purchase decisions lacks sufficient confidence to feel able to choose correctly.

And this is an important point; in inexperienced, usually independent, operations, brands play a very useful, powerful role in influencing decision making. Here, a retail brand with its widely promoted and understood positioning, brand values, and the rest is a powerful contributor to the decision.

But in those independent restaurants where the decision-maker is confident, and in group operations, the brand is not important, who cares about brand values, positioning, and the rest when the decision is going to be made on fitness for use, supply chain integrity (can I get the product day in, day out), price, provenance, and other technical considerations?

So for these people, while the brand may be helpful, the company behind the brand is much more important. It's not so much about buying the brand – it's about the company one is buying from. This might mean just having the right price, but, and this is the secret to securing long-term and profitable relationships in foodservice, the most fruitful relationships are where the supplier helps the customer to solve problems.

In other words, having a relationship with the supplier is far more important than a relationship with the brand. And a company that recognises this, and hires and encourages the kind of executive who understands this is better positioned to succeed in foodservice.

So, get to know the customer and sell your special capability to the customer, and job done! Well, unfortunately, no, the job isn't yet done, and that is for reasons which I'll go into later on. But it's enough for now to know that some orders – especially the larger ones -- require a relationship rather than a brand.

What has this led us to in terms of the role of your brand (or brands)? There are four points to mull over.

First, if you have a brand with 'magic' – by which I mean it has something unusual about it but is still aligned to the operator's need – then you have opportunities with a customer-facing, front-of-house offer. Like all things in this complex sector there are exceptions – but not many.

Second, in the front-of-house space, the brands of the cold drinks that are served – whether alcoholic or soft drinks – are very important. Sometimes they have an element of magic, but very often a recognised brand on its own is enough.

Third, group operators and confident independents don't need your brand – but they do need to buy from a reliable company, especially one with which they have some relationship.

And fourth, brands have an important role in inexperienced, less confident kitchens where the brand provides the confidence to back up an insecure decision. These are the minority in foodservice.

Bringing all these points together leads to the conclusion that, in foodservice, branding is less important than in retail. This means that you can spend less on your brand, and you'll therefore have more to spend on other things. This may not be an advantage though if the value of your company is in your brand (or perhaps brands), because you won't have the same opportunities to leverage the brand with its implications for premium pricing perhaps, or instant recognition and therefore a significant 'shelf appeal factor'. Indeed, if this is your positioning, you need to seriously consider your role in foodservice since the brand is, I argue, generally less powerful than the company it represents, i.e. your company. In foodservice you will have to invest in the company as a brand – featuring things like supplying practical solutions in the kitchen where effectiveness and fitness for purpose are important, or providing menu advice where your skill and expertise may provide answers to the operator's dilemmas, such as how to price, where to feature the product on the menu, what products to feature, how to describe the menu item, and more.

●

Is the brand king? *The brand is a useful foot soldier in food-service – the company is king.*

Cogs and levers

We've explored the essential character of foodservice and examined its relationship to the retail market for food. Now we should look at how and why it works. How do the cogs and levers, pulleys and flywheels, drive shafts and powertrains operate?

You may think that such a mechanistic view is not appropriate for something as relationship-driven as the foodservice sector. But these components are important, and by understanding them, you will be in a better position to see how what you do affects, and is affected by, all the other moving parts of this complex industry.

Multiple mechanisms are at work, and each mini-sector and distribution channel, even each operator and unit, has its own particular ways of doing things. But there are enough generalities – 'rules' even – to make how the whole foodservice system works understandable. The place to start is with the consumer. For simplicity, in this chapter I shall assume the consumer is a she.

Who eats out? A simple question with, at its heart, a simple answer – most people. And most people are still people who eat most of their food at home. In other words, people who eat out are the same people who shop in a retail store. The very sort of people your skills are aimed at.

So why should we consider these people separately in the eating-out environment when, after all, they're the same people whom you sell to and market to everyday in the retail environment? The answer is because it's more complicated than that.

To start, let's look at the core of people who do eat out. Some of them eat all of their meals out of the home every day. In this bucket I can put prisoners, the elderly, and others who are looked after in care homes. In this category, for simplicity, I'll also put people who eat out every day and who eat all their meals out of home, but only for a limited period, such as patients in hospitals or pupils in boarding schools.

People in these buckets have little choice over what to eat and no choice over where their food is served on a daily basis. Your efforts, as a supplier are, or should be, directed at the people who decide what is put on the plate and not who takes the food off it.

The next category of eater is the person who decides to go somewhere to do something – perhaps to watch a football match, visit a museum, go to the gym, or spend a few nights in a hotel. While there, they must eat. When faced with the option (or necessity) of eating at or near this location, the choice of where to eat may be narrow. And, in this bucket, the choice of food may not be very large.

But, consider the many options that can be found at a theme park or in a five-star hotel. In places like this, the customer can eat in many places in a restaurant, or at a fast-food outlet, in her room, or at a bar, or sometimes at a conference or a function. So, this bucket also includes options of what to eat as well as where to eat. And the lesson for you, in sectors like this, is that you should be working with the people who decide what options to offer consumers and where these options are offered.

My final bucket of three contains the majority of consumers who eat out – those who chose to do so. Here are just some of the reaons why.

She's going out to meet some friends – it's lunchtime and she works in central Manchester. She meets up with three friends in the centre, near Deansgate. This weekend she's going to have a dinner with her boyfriend and a couple they know well. They'll meet for a drink first before going on to a new Italian restaurant they've heard about on Facebook.

Meanwhile, her brother will be watching football on Sky – Man U versus City – and he's planning to order some pizzas from Domino's for himself and his mates. They'll buy the drinks beforehand at the local supermarket.

Her boyfriend's brothers plan to drink in their local and end the evening with a kebab from the takeaway before heading home.

Her father, an executive with an insurance company near Birmingham, is also having lunch. The restaurant at work is subsidised and offers a choice of light food and more filling hot meals, plus coffee, tea, and cold drinks, and snacks to eat there or at this desk.

Her grandmother who lives alone is having her lunchtime meal delivered by the local authority's meals on wheels service.

And in a couple of weeks' time there'll be a family get-together to celebrate her grandmother's 80th birthday, and her parents have arranged a lavish meal at a country club not far from where they live. And so it can go on and on...

All the many reasons for eating out can be boiled down into three main categories: refuelling – destination – and habit.

A refuelling meal is all about being hungry (possibly just peckish) and that now is the right time to have something to eat. It is usually planned – in a restaurant or at work, for example. But it also can be unplanned, perhaps in a pub while drinking where the sight of the menu induces hunger pangs.

Eating out as a 'destination activity', on the other hand, is a planned event – where the occasion can vary enormously from a couple's casual night out to a family celebration or Christmas lunch.

And finally, habit operates when you eat out 'because this is what I always do'– maybe at school if you are a pupil (or a teacher or an administrator) or Sunday lunch with the family at the local pub.

I have never come across any credible in-depth research that really explains how people make their eating-out decisions, but observation and discussion with many players, leading operators and independent operators, based in the UK, the US and elsewhere around the world, convinces me of several things.

The questions we ask when making our decisions are: Am I going to eat? Where am I going to eat? What am I going to eat?

Of course, these are not answered sequentially and not in a neat order either. And sometimes the questions don't get asked at all – in which case "I'll just do it – I'll just eat, here, and now". But even in these cases, the question is not totally ignored. For example: "Am I going to eat? It's lunchtime – so the answer is yes". Is that it? "Well no, not if I'm busy and just genuinely don't have the time – and my work pressure overcomes my need to eat. And no if ...". These are relatively trivial responses but go to show that our consumer asks herself these sorts of question but maybe she doesn't pay much attention to her answers. Impulse rules the decision. Similarly, "Where shall I eat? I always eat at .... but for once, and I'm going to be bold, I'll eat somewhere else". Again, this is trivial and the common factor behind apparently not answering the question is nearly always habit – this is what I always do – but always doesn't always mean forever.

So, what are the factors behind the answers to these three questions?

The first question, 'Am I going to eat?', is answered by considerations such as hunger or social dynamics – 'I'm with some other people and they want to eat even if I don't'.

The second, 'Where am I going to eat?', may be answered by necessity, 'I'm hungry and quite honestly there's nowhere else I can eat or want to eat', or others' wishes, 'I'm with a group of family or friends or business acquaintances; most of them – or the loudest – want to eat at this place'. Then there is availability – 'Here is somewhere to eat, why don't I pop in?' Or an response may be prompted by advertising and reputation – 'I've heard about this place – why don't I try it out?'

The last question is then, What am I going to eat? There is the cost question – 'Someone has to pay for what I'm about to eat. If it's me, I'll look carefully at the prices on the menu; and even if I'm not paying I'll pay some attention to what I think the payer wants to pay'.

Further drivers of what to eat can include the shape of my diet right now, or what I habitually eat, or perhaps some unexpected desire for the taste of something exotic. So, to the many reasons for choosing a venue and what to eat can be added other motivators – factors such as taste and diet will round out the decision.

Location figures in the decision mix as well, because our consumer's choice of where to eat may be driven by different motives at different times. She may have breakfast with a business contact, lunch with a friend, and an evening meal with her husband. She has put on many different 'consumer hats' in just one day and eaten in many different places. And tomorrow she'll put on more.

So when you look at people eating out in any one location, they will include people who have many reasons for their choice: you may be having a quiet meal with a friend, the next table is occupied by a raucous birthday party, and on the other side, there is mum, dad, and two bored kids. Each table – and each person at each table – has different needs

Within such a wide range of motives can we identify more commonalities? Indeed, we can, here are four.

The first is our consumer's need state. What is my state of mind right now? Is it receptive to eating out? Am I so hungry I'll eat almost anything, anywhere?

Then there is habit – do I always do this? At this time? In this place?

And to habit we can add what others think or say – in other words, social dynamics. What other people have told you before or you've read about online or seen in the papers, on TV, in a magazine, can influence the choices.

And finally, price: Can I afford it? Do I want to spend as much? Am I prepared to look mean in front of my peers?

So remember our three eating-out buckets: places where the customer has no choice over what to eat; places where the customer has choice over what to eat but, broadly not where; and places where the consumer has choice over where to eat and what to eat. Within these buckets are all these extra drivers and constraints. It's clear that the decision-making processes are complex. So, unlike the retail customer who shops at a relatively small range of shops (at least for food), our eating-out customer is unconstrained and is driven not only by her personal needs and objectives, but also by those of others too. And the places where people eat are equally difficult to categorise, because they are frequented by our confusing consumers with their very different reasons to be there.

Understanding the foodservice market is difficult; understanding why and how people make eating-out decisions just complicates things even further.

Who eats out? *People, all people, eat out. Each one goes to more than one, indeed many, eating-out spaces. People cannot be placed into eating-out silos.*

Who is in the money?

In this chapter we'll find out who makes money in foodservice – and how those people who make the money in foodservice differ from people who make the money in retail.

But before we get there, we'll have to do some investigating and get some terminology and a number of thoughts out into the open. That means we'll be spending a bit of time in this chapter looking at some fundamentals before we get to the answers that we're searching for.

And since we're talking about food let's start off at the beginning.

Whether we're talking about Alaskan pollack (which might or might not come from Alaska), strawberries from Kenya, beef from Argentina or Botswana, wheat from Canada, coffee beans from Colombia, or potatoes from Lincolnshire, we are looking at products that rely on the vagaries of the weather, the climate, the soil, the sea, or the air. Close involvement with these vagaries means that the farmers, or in some cases hunters, of these products are reasonably adept at forecasting quantities, costs, and quality outcomes. Of course, it's not always straightforward because floods, heatwaves, disease, and sometimes war can lead even the most experienced farmer to the wrong conclusions about what is going to be available, when, and at what price.

Making money at this level is difficult and exceedingly variable. That's why governments work hard to protect farmers from the unknown – much to the chagrin of taxpayers, politicians, and other competitors for government largesse.

The results of this planting, harvesting, slaughtering, hunting, and fishing are processed – they may be cleaned or perhaps frozen or shaped or graded or chopped – then transported. Maybe just a few miles or maybe halfway round the world. Here there are opportunities for freight transporters, whether air freighters or shipping companies or logistics companies, to make some money.

The freighted processed or semi-processed food is delivered to a factory or perhaps to a facility that will further process the product. This is where you, the reader, may well be located. You will be overseeing a plant that accepts raw materials – tankers of syrup or sides of beef or frozen fish slabs or one of the millions of kinds of food that are transported and delivered on an industrial scale to factories, large and small.

The next few steps are more or less programmed and generally controllable. Here there are several potential ways to make money. But the financial aspects here are driven by variable raw material costs and selling prices that are, in turn, determined by what the customer is prepared to pay. You, the manufacturer, have to do all the necessary processing at a cost that is less than the margin between the raw material cost and the selling price, two measures which are in many regards, immutable. You are always working between a rock and a hard place – somewhere between Scylla and Charybdis.

Efficiency becomes the name of the game where key drivers include technology, scale, and knowledge. Assuming you have these in the right balance, you, the food manufacturer, will be making a profit because you are spending less than the difference between what you pay for your raw materials plus your processing costs and the price your customers pay for your finished product.

The output of the activities we have just looked at now enter what many refer to as the 'food chain'. The gates of the factory or processor or the butcher or the dock open and let out trucks loaded with packets of soup on pallets, crates of sorted aubergines, yoghurt in pots. The list is seemingly endless.

We need to stop and look at the destination of these loads. One is to the retailer; the other to foodservice. The routes are different and the ways that money is spent throughout the processing and distribution chains are different.

The route to the retailer and beyond is what we're going to look at next.

The truck has left your factory and goes either to a central hub, or it goes directly to a store. The hub may be operated on behalf of a retailer and this, in the UK, is by far the most likely destination. But we shouldn't forget that it could be a hub operated by a third-party distributor – a delivered wholesaler or a cash and carry, that is, a middleman. This may be the most likely destination in many countries of the world (but not the UK). We'll look at these middlemen in more detail shortly.

But for now, we should assume that the lorry has arrived at the retailer's hub which has the responsibility of organising the movement of goods from factory to larder. It needs to do this in the most profitable way via transport to hub, transport from hub to outlet, transport within the outlet (along the way, minimising the amount of product that is not in transport – otherwise known as 'stock') and transporting product from the retail outlet to the consumer's larder.

So, the hub has a vital role in minimising costs, because it is here that the vast output of factories and processors is collected, stored, broken down into more manageable units, collated, loaded onto yet more trucks, and despatched.

Efficiency at this point is paramount and is moderately easy to achieve through (fairly high) investment in warehouse superstructure, technology, ongoing market intelligence, and knowledge about what's happening further down the supply chain. In other words, efficiency and systems rule. This is where costs are controlled and minimised.

The truck loaded with the products required by each store are despatched and become subject to multiple vagaries – traffic, weather, mistakes. But these can usually be managed; the costs outside what have been allowed for are small as a proportion of the total cost of delivery to the retail outlet. Nevertheless, there are costs in transporting product, and these costs depend on investment in vehicles, the people required to drive the trucks, fuel, maintenance, space for parking. and much more.

And here is another part of the chain where costs are minimised: The products arrive at the store and are delivered to the shelf in the most efficient way – minimising losses, reducing stock levels, optimising labour, and eliminating (if possible) mistakes. Human beings are involved at this stage and need to be managed so that they deliver the goods from the back of the truck to the shelf in the least costly way. Again, there are costs but they are controllable.

And now responsibility shifts from the retailer to the customer – at least it does under one model, where the customer visits the shop. And this activity is free. At least, it is free to the retailer (after allowing for the human costs involved in totalling up the purchases and accepting payment). There are costs to the customer – typically fuel – but this does not normally appear on anyone's profit and loss statement.

The food supply chain's job is now done? Well not quite, because nowadays, retailers may undertake to do the selection and delivery on behalf of the customer. So, for an increasing proportion of purchases, another element of cost has been introduced – the cost of delivering food (and other groceries) to the customer's back door. This is difficult to make money from because it is competing with a process that is free wherein customers select their products from the store and transport them home at their own cost.

But when the retailer (or its agent such as Ocado) does the delivery, there are costs, and because customers compare the costs against the non-cost of doing their own shopping, they are somewhat averse to paying for delivery which makes it difficult for the retailer to make an adequate financial return from delivery.

Let's sit down, catch our breath and tot up where the money is made. From earth, sea, and air, food is collected and processed. It is difficult to make money here.

The food is transported – sometimes short distances, sometimes long distances. This is a cost to the food processor or its customer. The processed food is further processed and turned into a packaged good of some sort. With the right investments, it is possible to make money out of this. There is additional transport to the hub and from the hub to the store. This is a cost to the retailer (or its supplier). And from the back of the store to the customer's back door – or larder – there are further costs to the retailer.

So, the trick for the retailer is to minimise costs and maximise sales. In the UK, the difference between costs and sales is usually 2% or 3% of the total sales value – it used to be higher, up to 7% or 8%, but competition, especially from low-cost retail models, have reduced the opportunity to make profits at levels like these.

So far so good (or if not exactly good, at least understandable). But you will, I hope, recall that I said earlier that we shouldn't forget that food could leave the factory gates and then be delivered to a hub operated by a third-party distributor – a delivered wholesaler or a cash and carry. In the UK, these distributors service the smaller retailer and not those retailers that operate their own hubs. This introduces another layer of transport and everything that goes with it into the distribution chain, and with this additional transport, there are, of course, additional costs. The net result is that retailers that use distributors find that their costs are higher than those that don't, and therefore either their margins will be narrower or their selling prices will have to be higher. Increasing prices is normally the route travelled by independent operators, but mitigated to a degree by lower operating costs (per unit of sale) based on lower premises costs (because the outlet is in a low-cost location, for example), lower overheads (no head office, for example) and lower salaries – the boss of an independent retail outlet is, sadly, by and large, paid less than the boss of a large retailer. The end result is that margins are similar to those earned by large retailers with central hubs.

So the key words throughout the retail sector are efficiency, cost control, investment in infrastructure, transport, and technology, and above all, minimising labour.

Now we can turn to foodservice. The truck has just left the factory gates, where does it go? Like the retail chain it probably goes to a central hub – but this will almost certainly be operated by a distributor and will not be a foodservice operator's hub. So the first point that becomes obvious is the importance of the distributor in foodservice, and as we have just seen that adds a layer of cost.

The foodservice distributor is in a fiercely competitive marketplace. Investment has to be made in warehouse space, backup systems, technology, and transport fleets;

and costs have to be incurred in sales, head office over-heads, and fuel. And because the end market, at the operator level, is somewhat chaotic, predictability is less than in the retail sector.

So, in this less predictable world, the distributor's job is to move things around efficiently, and because competition is rife and, although it needs investment on a breath-taking scale to become a large-scale distributor, costs of entry for those able to start small, are low. All that is needed is a man, a van, some storage space, some money for stock, and customers – net margins may be 3% at best.

The product arrives at the restaurant or pub or work place or wherever. And here is another crucial difference between foodservice and retail. In a retail outlet, the product is moved from lorry to shelf, and from shelf to customer. Simple and easy and crucially with minimal human involvement

In foodservice? The product is moved from delivery truck to larder (possibly chaotically and involving time spent in changing the layout of food in the freezer or on the shelf in the larder). The product may stay here for minutes or hours – or days or even weeks. Stockholding costs can be quite high. The product is then handed to the chef or some other food preparer. He or she cuts, chops, sauces, stirs, mixes, heats, cools, boils, grills, fries, and spends time and skill in turning the product that appeared at the back door into something that the customer wants to eat.

Unlike the retailer, whose job is to be an efficient distributor of product, the foodservice kitchen operative's task is to process food into something tasty that the customer will eat on the spot. That is another crucial difference between foodservice and retail, one that can be inefficient, wasteful, and costly. And costs have to be paid for.

And then the food has to be delivered to the customer – who has already taken up some of the waiting staff's time, and therefore has taken up some of their employment costs, in being seated, placing the order, and generally being looked after. This time incurs costs in the form of wages. These costs also have to be paid for.

So here is another crucial difference between foodservice and retail: it's the involvement of people who use their skills to deliver something, often something bespoke, to the customer. And that leads to added costs. These costs are generally at least the same as the cost of the food and usually somewhat higher.

Let's disentangle the costs a bit. First there's the food (and drink). For the retailer it accounts for about 80% of the final selling price that the customer pays, leaving 20% to cover all the overheads. The foodservice operator, on the other hand, spends about 30% of the final selling price on food and drink, leaving 70% to cover his overheads.

To be sure, the retailer has to pay for the labour it uses, but the labour cost is only a small proportion of the final selling price while, for the foodservice operator, it's typically a whopping 35% or 40%.

Now, when we put all these costs together we can see that the foodservice operator's costs break down into about 30% food (and drink), about 35% to 40% labour, and the rest is spent on overheads. And then compare this with the retailer's food costs of 80%.

And we can look at this in terms of gross profit – in other words, expressing the profit made on the cost of the food and drink as a percentage of the final selling price. When you do the maths, you can see that the retailer's gross profit is about 30% while the foodservice operators' gross profit is three times this, at 70%.

Or look at it another way and, rather than basing the maths on the profit made, base the maths on the amount spent on food. When you do this and show the food cost as a percentage of the final selling price, you'll see that the retailer makes 30% on the cost of the food – and the foodservice operator? He makes 300%. What's not to like?

Well, there is a fly in this particular foodservice oint-ment jar. And that is people; people cost money, people change their mind, people make mistakes, people don't turn up when they are supposed to. There are costs – and they are unpredictable. They eat up a big chunk of the foodservice operator's gross profit.

And before we go much further, consider this about foodservice, in the round, it makes no money!

Sure, some operators, indeed some complete sectors, make a profit – after all there is no purpose in running a restaurant or a chain of pizza takeaways, for example, unless there is a profit to be made. But some foodser-vice businesses can only operate at a subsistence level; the owners can take out something to live on each week only if they have money in the till to do so. The money may not exist one week, the next it may be plentiful, but overall it is small.

And much of the foodservice sector consists of outlets that provide subsidised food – hospitals, schools, perhaps workplaces, for example – and I have more to say on this subject later. By the very definition of subsidy, outlets that provide subsidised meals provide them at less than the cost of the food, labour, and other overheads involved in preparing and serving them. And as a result, revenue is less than costs – I am sure you will agree we can broadly refer to this as making a loss. And subsidised meals can include those like in-flight meals on airplanes which are not paid for at the point of consumption (a practice that is becoming less prevalent, however, at least on airplanes); and it probably includes the breakfast that you eat in a hotel but which you haven't directly paid for since it comes out of the cost of your overnight stay. This too, however, is changing as more and more budget hotels provide separately costed meals. Add to this 'loss making' subsidy model, the ongoing losses that bedevil some profit-oriented sectors, and the businesses that make a loss because they are less than perfectly run, and you have a foodservice sector that makes money in some sectors and loses it in others.

In overall terms, the profit and loss account is about zero. As I said, the foodservice sector makes no money!

And towering over all of these issues is competition and the willingness, or unwillingness, of customers to pay. And that essentially applies to what is perhaps with tongue in cheek called, by some, the 'profit' sector and the 'commercial' sector by others. This sector is populated by restaurants and pubs and fast-food outlets and similar places.

But a lot of food is served in schools and hospitals, at work, in prisons, to squaddies or to the house-bound. This is sometimes called the 'cost' sector because food is sold at or below cost. It's also referred to by others as the 'institutional' sector or the 'non-commercial' sector.

So, in operations such as these the food costs more to produce and serve than the income received? Yes, indeed: imagine a prison or a hospital where no money changes hands; or a school perhaps where the pupils pay something but not enough to cover the cost. Here subsidies rule – and they are usually provided by the 'authorities', generally (but not always) government, whether national or local, or some government-appointed body.

In summary then, we are looking at a whole swathe of the foodservice sector that is governed by crazy economics – where customers routinely pay less than it costs to produce and deliver what the customer has ordered. In this part of the market, making money is impossible, and frequently positively discouraged, and therefore costs have to be kept low. And they are kept low by, for example, buying cheaply or skimping on wages or failing to make necessary invesments.

In other sectors of the foodservice sector, the customer seemingly pays nothing for the food he or she consumes. Think, for example, of a meal served high above the Atlantic or breakfast served as part of an inclusive stay in a hotel. The air fare or the price of the overnight stay includes the cost of the food (or it should), but because the food appears to be 'free' the customer may overindulge, at the breakfast buffet for example.

Are the costs covered by the revenue? I only pose the question, because I have no genuinely comprehensive and realistic answer.

So, underlying the point I have made earlier, when you take the profits made in the 'profit' sector and subtract the subsidies applied to the 'cost' sector, we find that the foodservice sector as a whole makes no money. If you are a supplier, please bear that in mind when asking for the operator to pay for the goods you supply; be sympathetic to the point that 'on average' he is making no profit. And that is a big difference, between retail and foodservice, isn't it?

Within the foodservice operator's cost base, plenty of money flows to chefs, cooks, waiting staff, kitchen staff, and more. But this is the land of low wages, and although plenty of money is spent on labour in the foodservice sector (about £15-20 billion each year in the UK), the workers, individually, receive little because many are working at or perhaps only slightly above the minimum wage.

The margin cascade looks like this:

Price at the factory gate, or from the market or farm:	**£10**
Distributor's margin:	£ 3
Price at the operator's kitchen door:	**£13**
Operator's markup:	£26
Price on the menu:	**£39**
VAT:	£ 8
Price the customer pays:	£47
Plus, 10% tip (though the average is less)	£ 5
Total paid by the customer:	**£52**

So you can see how £100 of ex-factory goods is sold to the customer for 5 times as much.

At this point, I'd like to make an observation concerning the nature of commercial relationships, which in retail (because it is all about systems), are based on detailed and binding contracts. In foodservice these may be found in the largest deals between the largest operators and their suppliers. But, by and large, handshakes and understanding are the most common features underlying contractual relationships throughout the foodservice sector – and, of course, this ties in with its personal, hospitable nature. But things are changing so do not assume this as a given, even now – let alone into the future. Society is becoming more litigious which means that protection is sought by 'having it in writing'.

So let's return to the title of this chapter and finally ask: in foodservice, who does make the money? If it's not the food supplier, if it's not the distributor, if it's not the operator, and if it's not the worker?

Here are some people who do make money out of foodservice: property owners and their agents, lawyers, and shrewd investors who get into or out of the market at the right time.

Where is the money in foodservice? *Money flows to the efficient and the knowledgeable. Retail is not a helpful example.*

The Rule of One Third

Food is produced, processed, or manufactured – and much (but by no means all) of this is common to retail and foodservice. This activity is highly competitive and difficult to make money from; generally profits, such as they are, are made by the processor or manufacturer, and not necessarily by the farmer who may only be profitable through government intervention.

Food is transported – it is possible to make reasonable money here, but by the transporter not the food processor. Food may enter the wholesale distribution chain – modest profits can be made by the wholesaler. Profit may flow to the retailer who earns a 40% gross margin and a 3% net margin

Or it goes to the foodservice operator who earns a 300% gross margin and hopefully makes a small net margin – but no margin at all throughout the sector in aggregate as I've been at pains to point out.

Returning to the point I've already made about the breakdown of costs between food, labour, and other expenditure, there is a rule in the foodservice sector that goes like this: one third of costs are food and beverage; one third are labour, and one third are all other costs.

This applies wherever you look in reasonably developed foodservice markets. It applies across sectors, in restaurants, hotels, schools; and it applies in all countries, the UK, USA, Germany, The Gulf, Australia.

Why? It's driven by the major variable costs – food and beverage. If you, as an operator, don't sell anything, you don't need to buy any food (or drinks) to sell to your customers. If you have lots of business, you will spend a lot on these things. Clearly then, the amount you spend on your goods (otherwise referred to as your raw materials) will bear a very loose relationship to how much you sell – or more realistically it's the other way around.

So far so good. But of course, you have other costs. Some of these are fixed, rent for example, or insurance or the interest you pay on any loans. And much more.

The biggest of these costs is labour. As an operator, it goes without saying that you need to pay wages in order to get people to work in your kitchen and to serve your customers.

In practice, these labour costs are not totally fixed. Operators (canny, experienced ones, anyway) build flexibility into their labour costs by trying to match the numbers of people who work any one shift, or day, to the amount of business that they generate. The more customers they have, the more people they will have preparing and serving food.

In practice, though, employment costs are pretty much the same as the costs of food and beverage; and when they have added in all the other fixed costs, operators find that these 'other' costs come to about the same as their labour costs – or their food and beverage costs.

So, the maths shows that there are three classes of costs, all of which are broadly equal, and this means that each class amounts to one third of the total. Hence the Rule of One Third.

But that doesn't really answer the question why are these classes equal? The answer lies in the competition in the eating-out market. Costs of entry in many sectors are low, and competition is fierce. Customers can shop around and compare prices. And they do – all the time. It's what economists call 'a perfect market' where prices and costs are transparent (or at least reasonably so).

This rampant competition forces operators to offer their services at similar prices – at least in each sector of the market. Indian takeaways prices are similar, family pub prices likewise. Of course, this is a simplified picture since there are plenty of examples of operators who command a premium price, or undercut the competition. And at the top end of the restaurant sector, at least, prices are elastic, because customers will buy with scant attention to price. But for the majority of operators, price is an important driver of business.

This is not to say that customers only buy on price, but if an outlet charges higher prices, there has to be a good reason for customers to come in.

Competition, then, is important. And it drives the Rule of One Third in this way: first, operators, whether restaurant, takeaway, or pub, sell at a given price (because of competition). Second, food and beverage costs are variable but amount to one third of all costs. Third, the amount left for labour and other costs is fixed at twice the food and beverage costs (the maths shows this).

So, costs are squeezed into a straitjacket of fixed selling prices. If operators can't do this, either their costs will exceed their sales, or they won't get enough custom (because their prices will be too high). Either way, they will fail. If they succeed brilliantly, they will make big profits. But competition being what it is, and given low entry costs, soon a competitor will come along to reduce prices – and therefore profits

Thus, competition works in the foodservice sector and enforces the Rule of One Third.

But beware: the rule is flexible. The actual proportions vary across sectors – it applies pretty well in mainstream, full-service restaurants. But the balance tips in favour of labour in sectors with very high throughput – think of burgers, and takeaways generally. Or it can tip in favour of food and beverage costs in sectors where some of the other costs are subsidised. This can be an overt subsidy as in, say, workplace catering or in schools. But it can also be an indirect subsidy in pubs where the sales of alcohol on their own can, if the publican wishes, subsidise the cost of providing the food.

There are situations where the rule does not apply though. This arises when the customer knows the price of what they are purchasing (or has a pretty good idea of the price). For mainstream menu items – steak, pizza, burgers – the price can vary widely, depending on the location, whether the outlet is perceived as premium or downmarket or something in between, the value placed by the customer on added ingredients, and much more.

But consider a can of pop or a packet of salted nuts – generally these things that come under the heading of impulse purchase. Now not many restaurants sell things in this way, but plenty of coffee shops do or workplaces or kiosks at railway stations. The customer, faced with purchasing an item like this, is able to compare it with her knowledge of what the equivalent product costs in a shop.

Let's take a can of cola which last week was retailing at £1.10 at my local Tesco. Now I don't know what Tesco's markup is but let's say it's 25%. That means they buy it for 80p. Let's fantasise and assume that the caterer at your workplace buys it for the same amount (I say fantasise, because I suspect they are unlikely to match the price that Tesco pays, but we'll let that pass). If the caterer where you work applies the Rule of One Third, he will want to sell it for £2.40 which is way more than I bought it at Tesco's. With a difference of this amount, the consumer is going to say 'no thanks'.

So, what can the caterer do (or the coffee shop owner or whichever other operator is facing this dilemma)?

There are many options. For instance, he can decide not to sell the product, or the bottler can decide to sell a cheaper one, or the bottler could develop a larger pack or a smaller one making direct price comparisons difficult for the customer. But whatever the operator does, the Rule of One Third is going to make the product expensive – ranging from 'rather expensive', through 'very expensive' to 'outrageously expensive'. A price position of this sort might suit the operator, although it probably won't.

This forces the operator to sell at a lower markup than he or she would normally apply. Now there is not necessarily anything wrong in that. After all the purpose of the three times markup is to recover the costs of preparing and serving the meat or pasta or fish or whatever the dish is. For impulse products, there is generally very little in the way of preparation or serving. But the overheads that need to be covered are less. So in all honesty the operator should be willing to sell these things at a lower markup. But this goes against the operator's mindset and can rankle.

All things considered, operators work hard to find ways to price their menus and make a margin at the end. This is difficult with many moving parts on the menu. And the operator has to balance fixed costs, including for this particular argument, labour with variable and unknown demand. The Rule of One Third helps as a guide but can not replace careful pricing and accurate control.

How can I, as a supplier, help my customers price their menus and produce a profit? Be aware of the range of costs and their variability that your customers contend with – and design your products to minimise these costs.

How to get your
supplier to pay you

How often do you pay a customer – and what about suppliers who pay you? Welcome to the weird world of foodservice financial relationships.

In this chapter, amongst other things you'll learn when you will pay customers and when suppliers might pay you. To find out how and why these things happen, we'll have to delve a little bit deeper into a class of characters that we've already come across when we looked at some of the fundamentals of foodservice – this is the land of contract caterers.

These operators deal with businesses that have to provide food, but for whom this is not their main job. Think of a factory or an office, a school or a hospital? Their purpose is to make things or educate or heal. In doing so, they find that they have plenty of people who need to be fed – whether they are workers, students, or the sick. But for these businesses, feeding is very much a secondary activity alongside cleaning, gardening, mailroom services, and the front desk. Many years ago, businesses such as these started asking themselves why they should trouble themselves with providing food to their workers, students, patients – the many people who filled these spaces occupied by the business.

Would they not be better off focusing on whatever it is they are supposed to do and let someone else – a specialist – provide their food (or cleaning services and all the other things that they found they had to do but which didn't add much that was measurable to the output of the business)?

And they decided that they shouldn't do that those things if they didn't have to. So were born contract caterers. These businesses were set up at first just to feed people at work, and as time went by, they expanded their reach into schools, onto oil rigs, into care homes, and the other places I've already mentioned. And that's pretty much what they still do.

Now imagine yourself in their world. It is inhabited by a number of classes of players: there are the contract caterers themselves; there are their clients – the businesses and entities that need the services of the contract caterer in order to feed the people for whom they have a duty of care – their workforce, patients, students; then there are the actual customers, workforce, patients, etc., who eat the food. The final class of player is you – and your fellow suppliers.

So, how do they all fit together and how does money flow through the system? The starting point, as we've already discovered, is that site owners are transformed into the clients of contract caterers – in other words, site owners and clients are the same in this world. Clients develop relationships with contract caterers to feed customers.

Within this system, contract caterers don't own very much at the sites where they operate (although nowadays there is a strong tendency for their clients to demand that they make investments in kitchens and front-of-house operations).

But they do undertake to supply food to standards negotiated with their clients. By standards, I mean not only quality and price, but also range of cuisines, provenance, nutrition, and the other things that the consumer may want.

Clients provide the space and the customer. Thus, the system includes the customers who eat meals; the meals that are supplied by contract caterers; the contract caterers who reach agreements with their clients; the clients who own (or at least operate at) sites; the clients who 'provide' the customers to be fed the customers who eat the meals … and so the cycle continues.

Money changes hands or can change hands at the interfaces between customers and contract caterers, and contract caterers and clients – and indeed anywhere in the cycle.

The arrangements between contract caterers and clients are many and varied. But they all started out as a simple arrangement that arose out of a simple system. In those far off days, factories (and they were mainly factories) supplied food to their workforce. In time, for reasons that we've already looked at, they brought in contract caterers who were tasked with replicating the system that the employer had in place for feeding its workforce. And the contract caterers' remuneration was based on a proportion of the cost of the food – it was a simple case of transferring costs from one part of the P&L account to another.

Fast forward many years, and contract caterers became large and influential businesses, and the original system of remuneration became outmoded. New arrangements sprung up – and although they were varied, their main thrust was, and it still is, to transfer risk from the client to the contract caterer.

The purest example of this is the so-called full-risk profit model. The contract caterer, in effect, runs a restaurant (or perhaps coffee shop or fast-food operation) on a site that is operated by the site owner. The contract caterer takes all the risk – investing in front- and back-of-house equipment and services, paying rent to the client for the space that he (the contract caterer) occupies, and generally being a fully profit-centred business that happens to operate on someone else's premises.

And to highlight the role of the contract caterer, it is he who pays rent to the client and takes all the income from it.

Under this model it is vital for the contract caterer to provide just what the customer wants (like any restaurant operating on a high street). So, the contract caterer attempts to generate optimum profit, bearing in mind all the costs incurred and the income gained from the people who are on site. They may be employees in an office or patients, medics, and other staff, as well as visitors in a hospital or students or staff at a university – and multiple other customer bases.

Let's take time out here and catch our breath. In summary, the world of contract catering is a simple process in which customers pay to be fed by contractors, and these contractors (more usually called contract caterers) are paid (by customers and clients) for providing the food.

Along the way, it should be noted that clients may want the people on their site to pay less for the food than it costs the contract caterer. This is where subsidies reign – but they are not truly relevant to your view of the market except to say that the subsidy is paid by the client to the contract caterer.

And while we have spent some time looking at contract caterers, within the foodservice sector as a whole, another class of operator shares characteristics with contract caterers. The concessions operator inhabits a world where a landlord – usually a landlord with a very large site – operates a site that is enclosed. It may be very tightly enclosed, think airside at an airport – or it may have some natural boundaries – as in a shopping centre or a train station.

These sites may serve customers who come onto and leave quickly (as in a transport hub or a motorway service station) or customers who are encouraged to spend time and money (as in a shopping mall or leisure park).

Several factors operate in both types of sites. First, the customer's main purpose in visiting the site may not be (it usually is not) to eat. Second, as noted, customers may or may not spend time here. Third, the landlord wishes to increase the attractiveness of the site to attract potential customers. Fourth, the flow of customers is predictable (within reason). And fifth, the landlord is normally in it for the long term.

Now, many visitors to these sites do have time and the desire to eat. The landlord wants to attract people and has an offer – a regular flow of customers – to put in front of foodservice operators. So, the concessions business was born.

A concession is, in essence, a two-way deal between a landlord with its objectives of increasing revenue and profitability, and a foodservice operator who is seeking some form of guaranteed, or at least, predictable, demand. Concessions may be long term (25 years is not uncommon) so the operator has an incentive to invest in the site.

And all the while, the consumer, the visitor to the site, is being provided with another reason to visit and yet another opportunity to eat out. In the world of concessions, unlike the world of contract catering, the prices for food and drink that the operator expects to pay are the same as (or reasonably close to) the price expected for a site on the High Street, for example.

Returning to the mainstream description we are getting closer to the point which should interest you, the supplier. You will have noticed (I'm sure) way back in this chapter there was a point where I left three dots. They were deliberate. They occurred when I set out the chain of the contract catering system: customers – who eat meals – meals are supplied by contract caterers – contract caterers reach agreements with their clients – clients own (or at least operate at) sites – clients 'provide' customers to be fed – customers eat meals …

And I went on to say that money changes hands or can change hands at the interfaces between customers and contract caterer and contract caterer and client – and ...

You, the supplier, are the dots because contract caterers must buy food (and beverages) from you – the supplier.

And there is complexity here (this being foodservice, that is something you'd expect). As in normal commercial relationships, the buyer of food (the contract caterer) pays the supplier (you). Usually/often/sometimes, the contract caterer has a transparent, open book purchasing arrangement with its clients. The clients get to see how much the contract caterer pays for the food on their behalf. And usually/often/sometimes, the clients get a share of any discounts on offer on the food bought on their behalf.

The more the contract caterer buys, the greater his buying power, and therefore the greater opportunity he has for negotiating lower prices.

But the contract caterer has more than one client. So, its deals with you, the supplier, are based on the combined purchasing power from all clients. This buying power is, by definition, greater than the buying power from a single client. The contract caterer therefore finds that its buying power is enhanced.

Now who gets the benefit of the enhanced buying power? The contract caterer. And who pays? The answer is the supplier. So, in this world, your customer (the contract caterer) pays you for the food you supply, and then you pay your customer (the contract caterer) for all the additional food it buys on behalf of its total customer base.

And from the contract caterer's perspective, the supplier pays it (the contract caterer) some usually significant amounts, by way of overriders.

Payment in the contract catering space is complicated. Why? There are several links in the payment chain – each with its own rules and requirements. Spend time getting to understand them.

Contract caterers are the same as distributors

This is a very short chapter with a misleading heading.

In fact, contract caterers are definitely not the same as distributors – wholesalers, cash and carries, and other distributors. I have only used the title because of the number of times that I have been told by those with only a shaky hold on the foodservice sector that they operate through distributors like Bidfood and Compass. Bidfood is a food wholesaler and Compass is a contract caterer, and it is incorrect to conflate the two types of business. They do totally different things. Having said that, they do share some characteristics:

1. They include some big players; the biggest food-service players in the UK are in these categories.
2. The big players have the capability to become much larger especially through international expansion.
3. Their customers include large players in their own right.

4. They operate or service some very large, international contracts.

5. They are large buyers of food.

6. They buy a wide range of products.

7. They act in 'the middle', as a lubricant in the flow of business.

8. They act as honeypots for suppliers.

9. They demand – and get – the best prices from their suppliers.

10. They are demanding.

But their differences are more significant for you as their actual or potential supplier:

1. Contract caterers operate many kitchens often of no great size. Distributors operate a handful of usually very large warehouses.

2. Contract caterers don't drive anywhere. Distributors have fleets of lorries and other delivery vehicles.

3. Contract caterers transform your products (together with those of other suppliers) into meals for their customers. Distributors don't use the products you supply them with; they just sell them to another party.

4. Contract caterers make a gross margin of 300%. For distributors, it's 30%.

5. And above all – and please don't forget: Contract caterers make their money by feeding people. Distributors make their money by moving things around.

What is the essential difference between distributors and contract caterers? It is so simple: Distributors distribute – Caterers cater.

"Is everything OK"?
And what is the cost?

As we've already noted: the essence of foodservice is hospitality, and the essence of hospitality is making the customer feel valued and cared for.

And like everything in life, this comes at a cost. The cost in this case comes in the form of waste, because each customer is unique and has a multitude of needs and expectations. At any one time – say as the customer enters the restaurant or pub – there is no way of telling which of their needs and expectations will be paramount. Multiply this by the numbers of customers that come through the door in any single day, and it's clear that many unknown requirements must be met.

Of course, there are limits, someone entering a fast-food burger unit won't expect to be pampered, shown to a seat, presented with a menu of pre-prandial drinks, and offered hot towels at the end of the meal.

It is the job of the front-of-house team to make sure reality matches expectations. With the right skills and approach on the part of the management at the outset, the customer at a burger outlet can be made to feel as pampered as if she has been offered a hot towel!

The attempt to match reality and expectation carries on throughout the so-called customer journey, from entering the venue to the point of departure. And hopefully, customers will be satisfied more often than disappointed.

Now the point of this apparent digression is to underline that the unknown should always be expected in foodservice – and this calls for what the computer business calls 'redundancy', which is having too much back up resource 'just in case'. So it is in foodservice where 'just in case' is a way of life. It means, having pre-prepared fish ready in the fridge even though at the end of the day it may not have been asked for; it means ordering more gateaux from the local patisserie than cutomers order; and it means making more sandwiches at the start of the shift than customers who come in at lunchtime sweep off the shelves in the chiller cabinet.

'Just in case' can't be predicted; it is a built-in inefficiency, and inefficiency has costs.

So, the foodservice sector is inefficient; and noteworthy from your point of view, if you are steeped in the ways of retail, is that this inefficiency can be very expensive.

Now as a supplier you will be exposed to this inefficiency – through unanticipated orders, small scale changes, demand for help at short notice, and in a host of like ways. So, you'll have to face the fact that you will encounter inefficiencies – or as I will call it for now, 'chaos' – and you will have to face the costs of dealing with these inefficiencies and the resulting chaos.

From your perspective there are several practical outcomes. You need to have spare resources to deal with the inefficiencies; you must allow for unexpected costs; and you will have to find the patience to make your customer still feel valued through the chaos.

This is a fundamental difference from dealing with the retail sector where, although you will be called upon to meet special and unexpected needs, their scale and frequency are unlike those you'll meet with your foodservice customers.

Your corporate culture must understand and be able to deal with these foodservice needs and expectations otherwise your business will resent the costs and see the demands as unreasonable. And that can be a nail in the coffin of growing a successful foodservice supply activity.

You will have to have systems in place to manage urgent demands and changing minds, as well as understanding what timescale is acceptable – urgent might mean in the next hour or the next week or the next month. Remember that what might seem unreasonable to you might be perfectly reasonable, and in line with everyday practice, to your foodservice customer.

You have to get to know the foodservice business and its norms – and not assume that the retail market is a good template.

●

Why is foodservice inefficient? *The sector is based on human interaction and meeting human needs all the time.*

What is it?

What does being 'in foodservice' mean? What is a food-service operator? What are the essential functions of a restaurateur or a hotelier or a contract caterer?

We don't have to look far for the answers (in the plural because there is no single answer). And the first is quite close to home because home is where it's at. Just think of what running a home means. It involves several people – sometimes one of them is totally in charge, and sometimes it's a shared endeavour. Sometimes it works effortlessly, and sometimes it's a bit of a struggle. And the management of a home involves planning (when to eat, what food to eat, when to buy a new piece of equipment). It involves managing people (sometimes they don't do what they're asked), it involves cooking, cleaning, and a multiplicity of other tasks.

Ask a restaurateur or a publican or a dinner lady what they do, and they will essentially describe what is involved in running a home – they manage, they plan, they motivate, they do many tasks.

The next answer to my question, What does being in foodservice mean? is that it means running a factory.

A factory makes things to order, it tries to satisfy many needs at once, someone is financially responsible for its costs (and often that person is responsible for its sales too). It has to look carefully at what it spends, how it allocates its resources, and how to motivate people to do the tasks they are allocated.

In many respects, running a factory is like running a home on steroids, with the essential difference that running a factory is a transactional business where getting the job done is the key and the purpose. A home is a relationship business where, after all is said and done, the outcome is felt and sometimes measured in terms of how the people, who inhabit and use the home, feel.

And so it is in foodservice, which is like both a home and a factory. It needs to do things that are done in managing a home and mix them into the things that are important in running a factory while making people who are involved (as stakeholders, customers, users, and workers) do what is expected of them and feel great about doing so, and all the time controlling costs and maximising income.

And last of all, being in foodservice involves running and maintaining a business, that is employing techniques to maximize income. In other words, getting more customers to spend more money on more occasions. Of course, this also applies to retailers who deploy many skills – some more successfully than others – and the net result is they maximise their income. People in foodservice employ similar skills, and the result is that people in foodservice are like retailers. Some operators set this out explicitly – Domino's, for example, sets targets for new stores for customer traffic, they have targets for how much they want their customers to increase their expenditure every time they place an order, and they have targets for how much more often they want their customers to shop with them.

It all boils down to three drivers: more outlets, so greater opportunities to spend, more customers, so greater spending, and ultimately, greater expenditure per customer. Most foodservices businesses are less structured in their approach to marketing than Domino's, but these three drivers are, in my experience, present to some degree in most operators – and, dare I say, in all successful ones.

But it's not only this retail-based, strategic approach that foodservice shares; it also makes use of skills such as making the offer look attractive, getting the price right, satisfying the customers' needs – and then offering flexibility (making the offer match, precisely, what the customers thinks he or she wants).

Nowhere is this more explicit than in the front-of-house activities for those operations that are dependent on, or at least make great play for, impulse purchases. Here, I'm thinking about food-to-go offers particularly those aimed at a lunchtime crowd or people travelling by plane (think airports) or train (think stations) or by car (think motorway service areas). The operator often explicitly adopts a retail-type offer with products displayed in neat, orderly rows, with prices clearly marked, and additional offers, Meal Deals and the rest, set out clearly.

And this model not only works in the food- to-go space, but also for lunchtime feeding in outlets such as works restaurants and cafeterias, in museums, and in hospital cafes that are open to doctors, nurses, visitors, and, indeed, patients themselves. Fast-food operators also adopt a specifically retail-type approach in marketing their wares. You only have to look at their orderly queuing systems, offers set out in a manner that is clear and easy to grasp, and the efficient ways of taking money at the till.

So that makes three things that constitute a foodservice operator – running a home, running a factory and running a shop. I advise you to bear these three aspects in mind when developing your approach to foodservice – but then you have to take an extra step, because, as I have alluded above, while each foodservice operation shares these characteristics, how they do it and the extent to which they do it, vary.

So here is a simple exercise that I use with my clients who supply the foodservice sector; see how it helps you confirm your approach:

Step 1: Set down which aspects your business addresses best – running a home, a factory, or a shop. Note that I say 'addresses best', not just what you are good at. You may be good at several things – and your competitors may be good at them too. So in which things that you are good at do you outcompete the competition?

Step 2: Characterise the sectors that you sell into (or the sectors that you are thinking of selling into) into these three buckets – home, factory, shop.

Step 3: Set the answers to Step 1 and Step 2 alongside each other.

Now look at the results in Step 3 and see where there is the best fit – that's where you should hunt.

What is foodservice? *The answer is: it is running a home, a factory, and a shop. Concentrate on the one that works best for you.*

Complexity.
Where will you hunt?

One of the things commonly cited about the foodservice sector is its complexity – it is far more complex than the retail market – and that is often given as a reason for not bothering with the sector. But is that good enough?

First, it is very important to realise that this complex foodservice market in totality buys less food than Tesco alone. Just consider the retail grocery market. It's populated by multiple retailers – the so-called 'mults' – five companies whose combined purchases account for about three-quarters of the total. The rest of the market is occupied by smaller multiple retailers and independents. And while all of these come in a variety of flavours and trading styles, they are all nevertheless very similar. They will stock a similar range of products, and the brands will be broadly the same. But of course you also will recognise that own label sales are more significant for some mults than others. While upmarket retailers will stock brands that are more aligned with their upmarket position, value retailers will tend to focus on stocking value brands.

Retailers may differ in size, in opening hours, in location, in service levels, but the differences are not that great as far as the customer is concerned.

It's true there are differences in supply routes. The mults have cut out middlemen except for the logistics services that the middlemen provide – often referred to as 'wheels' – where payment is made for having goods delivered and where payment is made on the basis of volumes that are dropped and not by the value of goods supplied. Smaller retailers, lacking the size to help them access the buying power that combined purchasing can generate for the mults, use delivered wholesalers or cash and carries, but basically there's a fairly straightforward ordering and delivery process.

Now consider foodservice where complexity reigns. Is a coffee shop similar to a care home? Or a pub like a prison? The differences appear to be, and in actuality are, vast. So, there is truth in the statement that the foodservice sector is far more complex than retail.

The complexity can be managed and when it is. it can yield opportunities. That is the topic I'll be investigating in this chapter.

There are nine sectors within foodservice – don't just take my word for it but look at the definitions used by many of the major players. These nine sectors are: (full service) restaurants, (quick service) restaurants, pubs, hotels, leisure, staff feeding (often referred to as business and industry), health care, education, (public) services.

I created this typology in the 1980s, and it is now followed by most operators and industry observers when they report on the whole foodservice market. And that is because it provides a simple-to-understand view of the market and yields sectors of roughly similar size (except for (public) services, which as a category is considerably smaller than the rest).

But it wasn't originally like this. When I started to look at the foodservice sector around 40 years ago, there were no definitions; so I created them. I initially identified about 20 sectors, too many to graphically display and summarise and give a reasonably comprehensive overview of the market in a simple and readily understandable way.

So I decided to combine sectors. For example, hospitals were one sector, care homes another. Combined, they made health care, a sector that is defined by the fact that most people being fed in the sector are in less than perfect health, they are fed three times a day, funds generally are low, they have specific requirements from the food they eat, and similar factors are at play. Thus, hospitals and care homes form a coherent whole. But they are also different – for example, some of them are run in the state sector, others are privately run, while others are run by charities. They range in size from large teaching hospitals to the smallest of care homes. So, it is also important to be able to split sectors into component parts.

In fact, nowadays I split the nine sectors into a total of almost 100 sectors and subsectors, and then I further define them by style of ownership (group / chain or independent) and how they are run (whether contracted or run in-house). Thus, in my reckoning, when you take all the potential definition points into account, the foodservice sector should be separated into about 400 different categories!

And I'm supposed to be arguing that the sector is not complex? Well actually, and as the last few paragraphs have demonstrated, it is very complex. However, there are simple solutions to this complexity when it comes to defining the market. The 'nine sectors' view is one way to reduce complexity. But there are more subtle ways too.

Let's imagine that you supply cereals or orange juice or bacon or eggs. Clearly, you will be interested in breakfast. And to simplify your job, you may be looking at sectors where breakfast is a major component of the profile of its meals. Hotels fall into that category (including bed and breakfasts, of course). So, do hospitals and care homes. And then there are boarding schools (and you could also possibly be interested in prisons).

In hotels, breakfast accounts for about a half of all meals served (actually usually somewhat less, for technical reasons, such as the feeding of staff who don't require breakfast). In most sectors (apart from hotels) that are expected to serve breakfast – hospitals, boarding schools, prisons, and the like – breakfast accounts for about one third of all meals, and that third arises because the people who populate each of these sectors are on the premises for much of the day. This applies to the people who are the subject of the service being provided (for patients, pupils, even prisoners); it applies slightly less to the people who make the place run (administrative staff, nurses, doctors, teachers, and the rest). But, on the other hand, it may include serving some other people on an intermittent basis, such as visiting dignitaries in schools and visitors in hospitals. But putting this detail aside and combining these sectors gives a potential breakfast market in 70,000 or so outlets in the UK, and they buy a combined £1 billion worth of food and beverages for breakfast.

That's a substantial market, and one worth focusing on if you have the relevant product range. And that, in turn, argues for defining a sector where 'breakfast is very important' or some such. And this doesn't acknowledge the many other places where 'breakfast is less important' – coffee shops, some pubs, some restaurants and more. Adding in the breakfast meals that are served in outlets such as these, adds considerable heft to your ability to expand your opportunities.

Or perhaps you want to focus on sectors where alcohol is important – maybe you supply a complimentary product, savoury snacks for example, or perhaps you supply an innovative alcoholic product. Your interest then will not only be in pubs, but also in hotels (or at least those with bars), restaurants, and student unions. This is a market worth £4 billion or so at the level of food and beverage purchases (and that excludes all the alcohol and soft drinks that are served without food in these places).

By now, although I hope I have convinced you that complexity in the foodservice sector can be managed, it is still true that foodservice is more complex than retail. Unfortunately, complexity is not only a function of differences between sectors, it can also arise from differences in size.

Within the foodservice sector, about 260,000 outlets provide the product (actually, of course, the service) that we call foodservice. Their combined food purchases are only about 15% of the combined food and beverage purchases of the retail sector – and remember, the whole foodservice sector buys less food than Tesco. So, volumes in foodservice are small and numbers of buying points are large when set alongside the retail market, which means that complexity is baked into the way the foodservice sector buys.

So, when you gear yourself up for launching into the foodservice sector, make sure you understand not only the degree of complexity but also the nature of the complexity. And make sure you have a plan, or plans, for dealing with the complexity as it impacts on your business prospects.

However, that is not the end of the story. I am often told by suppliers that they can get higher prices in foodservice, and therefore by implication the margins are higher too. But just think about how the customer spends his or her money when eating out. The average amount that they'll spend is of the order of £15 – although it may be as low as £3 and in some high spending restaurants, it can be in excess of £150. What can you get for £15? The answer is: some protein (meat or fish for example), some carbohydrate (flatbread perhaps, or a bun), some vegetables, salad, etc., garnish, sauce and some items on the side, plus a starter or a dessert or both. I'm not about to decry the value, but I am going to compare this with what the same customer may be buying in the supermarket – just look at the trolley full of packaged, canned, frozen, chilled products. And look at the queues waiting to check out. And compare that with the possibly 100 people who will be served in a restaurant in the course of a day, each requiring less than half a kilo of food.

A crucial difference is in the run lengths – the volume of goods (whether measured by weight or in cases or in pallets or in some other way) – that your factory needs to produce in order to satisfy the different demands of the customers for the product that you supply. The run lengths in retail are large and extend along the supply chain from your raw ingredient suppliers to your factory, and in the supply chain that you run to your customers. Production lines are designed with the required run lengths in mind. The run lengths in foodservice are small and, in essence, only extend back from the table to the kitchen – from front of house to back of house.

And the run lengths you are required to provide through the sales you make to foodservice operators are made even smaller by the need for each operator to appear to be different from their competitors. Remember, they are not selling your brand, they are buying from your company to enhance their brand.

So, each customer may require something different, and each iteration of special requirements calls for shorter runs. The result is higher costs – and higher costs that your customers (and their customers, the consumer) may be reluctant to pay for which negates, in part or completely, the common argument that foodservice is more profitable.

What all this means is that the high foodservice margin is eaten into and the apparent profitability available to suppliers is no longer there.

●

How is it possible to reduce complexity in foodservice?
The complexity can't be removed – it's part of the system.
But how you deal with it can be improved. Use experience;
define what you're talking about; narrow your horizons so
that you do not have to understand it all.

Question your motives

Given the complexity of the foodservice market and the resulting sheer effort needed to push 'product' through the system, what is it about foodservice that is alluring? And why do you want to follow the rainbow? These are perhaps the most important questions you can ask, so please think carefully about your answers. You can easily be in danger of making a big mistake if you pursue your goal without being aware of the implications – and if you make decisions based on shaky foundations.

In my extensive experience, supplier companies are in foodservice or want to get into it (in other words they already supply the foodservice market or would like to) for one of two kinds of reasons. The first are emotional, and the second are practical. So, let's unpack them.

Emotional reasons often centre around the fact that foodservice is somehow actually or is seen to be sexier than retail. It's the focus of television programmes, it's a topic that our friends are very happy to have an opinion about, we have more fun in a restaurant than in a shop, and for a lot of other, but similar, reasons which lack rationality.

Or reasons may be based on negative emotions. Typical is the view that 'I don't want to be held to ransom any longer by arrogant retailers who don't appreciate me or the efforts that my company makes day in and day out to accommodate their unreasonable demands'. If these kinds of reasons are motivating you, please be aware that that is what is happening.

Practical reasons for being in or getting into foodservice can be based on many considerations. For instance, you may have excess capacity. Or you are building a new storage area that needs filling, or you are investing in new production kit for the retail market but it won't be profitable until volumes build up to a level – and additional business from foodservice can provide the production or storage boost that's needed. These can be valid reasons. But please, please make sure you are aware of them, because as part of your decision-making process, you are probably going to accept that the additional foodservice business does not have to be too profitable, or maybe it doesn't have to be profitable at all, so long as it pays its way. That's fine as a starting point – but as business builds and you start to fill your capacity, arguments over low, or no, profits should fall away. And they usually don't disappear, because you will become concerned about losing business if you raise prices to gain profitability. So, make sure that any negotiations that involve filling the factory allow you to change your price structure and don't lock you into a fundamentally unprofitable deal. Be careful is what I'm saying.

A frequent reason given for entering foodservice is that it's growing or it's large or it's profitable – or all three. Again, be careful if your arguments are based on any of these claims. And over the next few pages we'll find out why.

Claim number one is that foodservice is growing (and retail isn't, or it's only growing slowly). While this book isn't intended to show you historical changes in this market and its growth or lack of it, I'll just present one example.

The number of meals served out of home in 1944 was well in excess of 10 billion – and in 2016 – seventy years later – what was the figure? According to my research, 8 billion meals were served in 2016. That was a decline of 2 billion meals – and that's certainly not growth.

So, growth is not a given, but it's instructive – I'd say it is essential – to look behind these numbers and learn three lessons.

First, consider the national context in 1944. Britain, along with most of the rest of the so-called advanced world, was at war. War requires men and women in the armed forces, and it needs to mobilise large numbers of people to do things like manufacture armaments. The war in 1944 required women who had not ever worked outside the home to fill the occupations on the land, in factories, and offices to replace the men who had been called up. In this way, in 1944, the armed forces and the rest of the working population included over 7 million extra people – requiring an extra 6 billion meals a year. Some of these were served to forces overseas. So, lesson number one: compare like for like – and recognise, as in this example, that the picture in 1944 was not like the picture in 2016.

(In fact, in the years after 1944, the number of meals eaten away from home in the UK fell steadily throughout the later 1940s, the 1950s, and well into the 1960s. They only really started to grow again in the 1970s.)

Next, let's look at the 'shape' of the market. In 1944, the armed forces, along with feeding in works canteens, plus feeding children at school and other government-sponsored institutions, such as luncheon clubs and so-called 'English restaurants', accounted for 80% of all meals eaten out of home. In 2016, it was 40%. So, over this period of 70 years, the pattern of eating out has changed fundamentally – in 1944, meals in pubs, cups of coffee taken at a coffee stall, and the mainstays of today's eating-out market hardly made a dent in the numbers – but fish and chips certainly did, forming, as they did, the cornerstone of the culinary habits of swathes of the population, especially in disadvantaged coastal areas. So, lesson number two is that growth is not the same everywhere, and since your products are not going to be suitable for all eating-out places, your potential growth is not going to be the same as any overall growth that the sector experiences. Your growth potential might be less than the overall rate of growth; of course, it may be more – and I hope it is.

And a third lesson is that nowadays the eating-out market is far more mature than it was in 1944. That means change is going to be fairly small year on year – even at the height of the great foodservice recession in 2008–2010, the numbers of meals only declined by 2% a year, and the value, even in real (inflation-adjusted) terms, fell by just over half of this because of a shift in market share, away from lower cost, government-sponsored and financially supported feeding (in schools and hospitals especially), to higher margin, profit oriented, casual dining, and fast casual meals.

The corollary of this benign pattern of decline (when it occurs) is that growth, when it arrives (as it always does after a downturn) is equally slow – or should I say sluggish. I've already said the foodservice market is mature, and, as anyone who notices they are growing old will tell you, maturity brings slower growth.

So far then, we have learned three lessons: one, when looking for growth in the foodservice sector, make sure you are comparing like things – pears may be growing while apples are falling! Two: growth is not the same everywhere – and in foodservice, rapid growth somewhere, say in coffee shops, frequently means a decline somewhere else, say in community pubs. Three: change is slow, and expansion is generally sluggish in foodservice.

The conclusion is that arguing that foodservice is a potential sector for growth can be misleading unless you know these facts and build them into your thinking and conclusions. However, note that growth can be a powerful argument for you if you are going to target high growth sectors – they exist, even though they can be hard to find sometimes and are often quite small.

Another reason that many companies put forward for thinking about starting to supply the foodservice sector is that it is a large market. Well, how large is it?

Let's start off with a review of the size of the market we're addressing. The sales value of food eaten and beverages consumed in the UK foodservice sector is about 30% of the sales value of the retail food market. In the US it's nearer 50%, and in no other country with a developed foodservice sector, is it anywhere near this half-way mark. Back in the UK, after the great foodservice recession, the market was worth about £50 billion valued at the prices that consumers paid, and since then it has been growing slowly both in real and nominal terms, i.e. with and without adjusting for inflation. The definition I have used excludes some things such as alcohol consumed in pubs, hotels, and one or two other places without any accompanying food, and it excludes confectionery and savoury and other packaged snacks that people might buy from a shop and then eat, but not at home. Adding in things like these, the figure comes to about £70 billion or so.

I prefer the lower figure because it accords with what most people (other than suppliers of alcohol, cold drinks, and savoury snacks) consider to be foodservice. So let's take £50 billion as the value of the foodservice market in the UK.

Food sales account for about £35 billion of this – and, bear in mind, this is the amount that consumers spend. Foodservice operators work on a high markup on their costs of goods (in this case, food); we've already noted that the figure is about 300% – and that means operators spend about £11 or £12 billion on food which they transform into sales of £35 billion to their customers.

They'll buy their food mainly from middlemen (wholesalers and the like), and when we allow for their markup, we are left with a figure of £8-9 billion for the value of food that leaves the factory (or farm, or market, or processor).

In other words, the total foodservice market for food sold by you (assuming you are a food manufacturer or added-value processor, such as a butcher) is £8-9 billion a year. I leave it up to you decide whether that constitutes a large market – and your answer may well depend on the answer to a further question, which I don't have the space to answer here: What is the foodservice market worth for the food category that I sell?

And the third main reason that suppliers give for entering the foodservice market is that it is more profitable than supplying retailers. Well, what is the reality?

There are going to be significant costs. There might be the costs of building a brand, such as researching and implementing its positioning, the costs of the necessary production plant, and the costs involved in gaining consumer recognition. Just building a retail brand involves other costs such as product trialling, pricing differentials, and more. However, in the world of own label supply, costs are likely to be much less. Check whether your foodservice business carries (or is expected to carry) its share of these costs.

Likewise, the retail sector requires new products – on an ongoing and, for some products, on a significant scale. Check your company's accounting structure to see if your foodservice business carries (or is expected to carry) its share of these costs. Of course, there may be good reasons for not carrying this share – perhaps the cost of investing in new product development is not required in foodservice especially if it only involves minor changes that may not be significant for the food-service sector.

Large foodservice accounts require fewer people to be involved in client handling, and therefore call for lower client management costs than are needed to handle a large retail account. This is a slippery concept because, for many accounts, the size of the resources deployed are not up to the task of efficiently coping with the needs of the large account. The people will be up to the task, but the income may be insufficient to carry any more management in the form of people overheads. But in general, account management costs for foodservice are less than in retail where there are often large teams to manage individual accounts.

And here is another difference when comparing the comparative resources need for foodservice and retail: there is no point in using mass media for foodservice – TV, national press, etc., – because specific coverage of buyers in the foodservice sector is inadequate, and anyway, operators expect to learn about products and companies through trade channels. These channels include wholesaler catalogues and price lists, as well as participation in trade shows and learning from field sales forces. Activities such as these cost less than the mass media options generally needed to reach the retail customer. Of course, social media and the internet are changing these equations rapidly and significantly, but the foodservice sector, being slower to adapt to these modern media, still relies on the old-fashioned, less tar-geted, and arguably more expensive trade media. This will change, but slowly.

While your margins may be higher in foodservice (and bear in mind they may not be, so check this), the level of sales will almost certainly be substantially less than in retail. This means that while the profits in foodservice measured in percentage terms may be higher than in retail, measured in £ profits, they may be less.

So, you may want to be in foodservice for a variety of reasons: Because it's growing – but is it? Because it's large – how large is it? Because it's profitable – but is it? This leads on to questions about your corporate expectations for foodservice. In my experience there are any number of reasons why a supplier supplies the foodservice sector and I'll enumerate some of the commonest here.

Number one is: 'We've always been in foodservice, it's a formal part of our business, it has its own P&L and the rest'. Fair enough and usually a good enough reason. But ask whether it's profitable, or at least sufficiently profitable for your requirements. You may have lost sight of this over the years.

The second reason for being in foodservice is: 'We're in foodservice, or we're going to get into foodservice because it's profitable'. But is it? Use some of the insights above to check.

Reason number three is: 'We're going to get into foodservice to help fill our factory / new production line / pay for our additional storage capacity'. This is fair enough for the short term, but check whether it's going to work out in the long term. I say this because using this resource-filling argument, you will be happy to work in foodservice at, or even below, cost because of the financial uplift it will provide to the corporate whole. But as foodservice grows, the lower prices, and therefore your lower profit expectations, will become baked into your system and will, ultimately, become a drag on your corporate viability. All I say is: be careful.

The fourth reason is: 'We've got hold of a number of foodservice accounts over the years – they are somewhat random like a sandwich chain and a pub operator plus a couple of mid-sized hotel accounts. It makes sense to bring them all together and give some substance to the structure of this part of our business'. Fair enough but please bear in mind the costs involved.

And fifth, people say, 'We are encouraged by our owners in the USA/Europe/China or elsewhere to get into foodservice. It works in their country so why not over here'? Just check that this argument compares like with like. Are the products similar? Is their foodservice market structured similarly in the UK? Superficially, 'getting into foodservice' might be a useful headline, but the details matter more.

And the sixth and final reason that people give me is: 'We want to use the opportunity to try our product in foodservice as a way to enhance retail sales and profits'. Again, fair enough. But if this reason is merely being used to support a retail marketing proposition, then treat it as such and make sure that your retail arm pays for the benefits it's going to gain.

In summary, please question your motives for getting involved in foodservice. Examine your assumptions, especially around costs, and only when you are satisfied that your reasoning and assumptions hold up, should you be ready to make the moves that will commit you in foodservice.

Why am I in foodservice? *This is a crucial question, and you must be honest with yourself on this because it will drive your behaviours – in terms of pricing, positioning, profit expectations, and all the rest.*

Managing a category

In the retail world, one of the skills that has become important over the last twenty or so years has been the ability to develop plans that exploit the desire for choice.

Customers want to be offered a choice when making a purchase decision. The choice may be between competing products (coffee or tea), between pack sizes (small, medium, large, extra-large), flavours (mild, strong, fiery), price (cheap, mid-price, expensive, premium) and more.

Coping with this desire for choice demands an understanding of the category, whether hot beverages, men's toiletries, or frozen potato products. So, a complete information and consultancy industry has grown up to define what each category comprises, what the key measures are, how best to examine the category, and who the players are. And then to define (relatively) simple rules that will help retailers manage their categories – which brands to stock, which packs (sizes, formats) to stock, which prices, and how to display and merchandise products and brands in this category.

Retailers do this work themselves, but they also rely on (generally at no cost) their suppliers to provide the required information, insight, and plans. This is a clever, if well-worn, move by retailers since suppliers in their eagerness to work with retailers are prepared to do this at no cost – and retailers exploiting this keenness, generally pick just one supplier in each category to provide this work for free.

But make no mistake, this is a significant cost to bear for suppliers to the retail sector. And it also applies in foodservice.

It is helpful to recognise distributors as well as retailers must supply a range of products (i.e. choice) for their customers. In essence, this requires category management skills and a range of techniques which foodservice distributors have been able to bring in from the retail market. And just as in retail, so in the world of foodservice distribution, suppliers fight for the privilege to be appointed a distributor's category champion with all it implies in terms of a close working relationship with the chosen distributor and the ability to influence what products are stocked and offered to customers, and at what prices.

But the position of category management is somewhat different when we look at foodservice operators rather than the distributors that they chose to buy from. Operators engage in category management when they construct their menu – perhaps three starters, one fish dish, three meat dishes, a burger, a pizza, two vegetarian dishes, four desserts. In other words, the operator has made category choices in creating and designing the menu.

As a supplier of tofu or fries or tomato paste for pizza, you might be able to help the operator decide the best product for his or her needs, but the operator is unlikely to want you to apply your category management skills to his menu.

An exception is in the drinks area, especially alcoholic drinks where specialist suppliers, in wine, for example, can be a source of real knowledge and advice for food-service operators. And there are other examples; this is the world of foodservice where exceptions are the rule – such as breakfast cereals in hotels or cheese for serving on cheese platters.

But back of house in the kitchen where the menu has defined which categories are to be used and which products are to be offered, the chef will buy products that are fit for their intended use. He or she doesn't need to, indeed won't want to, buy a range of ingredients of a similar type for each dish. They will just buy the best for what is required. Operators may use several types of sauce but only a single one for each application.

So, category management in foodservice is a skill which you can deploy straight from your retail experience and apply to your dealings with distributors. But operators themselves will be much less likely (and that's putting it mildly) to want to deploy a category, either in the kitchen or in front of their customers. So, tread carefully when you talk 'category'.

Why is 'category' an alien concept for operators? Because they buy on the basis of fitness for use and not on offering the consumer a massive choice.

Compliant customers

Wouldn't it be great if your customers did exactly what you want? Well of course, they never do and that's just a fact of business life. Your skill, and probably in the end one of the factors behind your success, is your ability to get customers to do what you'd like them to do while giving them the feeling that you are doing exactly what they want you to do. In other words, you'd like compliant customers

But compliance also means doing what you say you'll do – or more specifically for my topic in this chapter, getting customers to do what they say they will do. Promises may be made but not kept. Or you may take what your customer views as aspirations to be promises, while your customer treats them merely as informal undertakings or even just as wishes.

For example, after superhuman efforts on your part, your products or your company might get listed as a supplier by a contract caterer. Job done, just let the orders roll in.

Well unfortunately not. The caterer has not really promised to use your products; all that has happened is that you have agreed on a price, and probably come to an arrangement over service levels that will apply should the client decide to buy your products. You may think that this is just a simple matter of ensuring that the person who specifies the product actually buys it. But, contract caterers, just to take one example, do not have a single person who specifies what product to use. Decisions about which product to buy may be pushed right along the chain to the unit manager or to the chef at each site.

So, we get to a point where you have agreed, with some central bargainer, the conditions for supplying your product, but getting compliance throughout the customer's business will still be, from your perspective, a continuous process that requires further ongoing selling to the individuals who specify the product; and, as I have already pointed out, this can extend along the chain to individuals working right at the coal face – the manager or the chef.

Don't think this only applies to contract caterers. It applies in hotels and pubs and throughout the non-commercial sector. In fact, the only area where it doesn't apply is in those customer-facing operations where central control is there to ensure consistency throughout the brand and its estate, and amongst franchisees. Customer-facing brands that fall into this category typically include fast-food chains and food-to-go operators – burger chains, coffee shops, pizza chains, and more, especially where franchisees are found, and those casual dining chains which strive to provide consistency wherever and whenever you dine at one of their outlets. In these places it's the same experience, the food is the same (or at least the menu is fairly similar), and prices are consistent.

Outlets which follow head office directives to the letter are, in effect, few in number – perhaps fewer than 40,000 units out of the 260,000 that make up the foodservice sector. The rest are independent operators where decisions are, by definition, made at the outlet level, or non-compliant group operators where you have to go to the coal face to secure the order.

What does all this mean to you? There will be higher costs – like the cost of getting your products specified and the costs of keeping on top of each of your customers' changing store-level decisions. Please bear in mind that these decisions can change for many reasons – perhaps a new manager takes over or the chef changes. Or, maybe a local competitor has started to do something that seems worth copying (or steals some business). The list is long and the changes constant.

So, when you prepare your P&L budget for the foodservice sector, please make sure you have a line that accounts for ensuring compliance.

Getting accepted by the customer as a supplier, with all terms agreed, is not the time to relax. It's when you need to ramp up your involvement with the customer to reinforce the opportunities for gaining the business.

When will you deliver?

More importantly, this chapter should have been titled 'How will you deliver?' Throughout this book I have written as if you are in constant, if not daily, touch with your customers.

In reality. this just doesn't happen. There are just too many touch points – 180,000 places where decisions are made and millions of consumers to influence.

There are accounts that can be worth devoting a lot of resources to – but they are few and far between. For example, the largest fast- food chains – think McDonald's – buy large, very large, quantities of product. But the range is limited. If you are in the happy position of supplying companies like this, you will want to, and you will probably be able to, justify devoting resources on daily, even hourly, contact with the people in the account company.

At a slightly different level, contract caterers buy large quantities – even though compliance may be an issue – and again, if you are supplying them, you will (I hope) find it justifiable to afford regular and frequent contact with the account. The same sort of thinking can also apply to a number of accounts in other sectors too – chain restaurants, food-to-go brands, and pub operators are all typical examples. But there are not very many of these – a few hundred accounts of any size, at most. And because there are few of them, and because they are relatively easy to identify, you will find that your competitors will also be feeding off the same honey pot, making customer contact a core requirement while prices are being driven down.

And then added to these large accounts, there are smaller operators who come in multiple shapes and sizes and with whom you may have a close relationship – perhaps because of luck, or maybe you have been supplying them since they were a small start-up, and they believe that loyalty counts for something.

But you will find that the most accounts will be small and it will be difficult to maintain a close, and definitely costly, relationship with all but a small handful. What do you do about that?

Before answering that question, just let me summarise: there are a multitude of foodservice accounts but few are of any significant size – and it's pretty obvious that you won't have the financial, human, or other resources to deploy the 'correct level of contact' (whatever that correct level is).

So, a key question arises: How do you deploy your finite resources to maximise your opportunities? This is where distributors step up to the mark. I am talking about what used to be called 'middlemen' then 'wholesalers' and now 'logistics'. But for deploying your limited resources, the first term is most appropriate: you need a middleman – someone, some organisation, that acts in the middle to bring you and your customer together.

The middleman – who may be a delivered wholesaler or a cash and carry (or in some instances, could also be a sales agent or importer) – is your channel to the parts of the foodservice sector that you can't reach on your own. The middleman is the pipe through which you communicate with the world of foodservice.

Let me add a very important caveat here which I hope you will cut out and stick on your office wall: although the middleman may also be a wholesaler and may also include a logistics function, this is not always the case. And you should be aware – and explicitly state on the piece of paper that you will by now have stuck on your wall – what is the purpose your company has in dealing with these types of businesses? Is it just to get your message to the foodservice operators that purchase your products? Or is it to provide the physical channel from your factory to the operators' larder, i.e. logistics? And if it is a combination of these, how important are they, in your particular case, to your customers – and to you?

The businesses I am talking about here, will sell your product – either with your best interests in mind (that's the role of agents and brokers) or with their own interests at heart (that's the middlemen who take title to the goods that they sell; and they include wholesalers, and cash and carries. Or perhaps your customer's interests are at the forefront of their minds (and I'm now talking about logistics companies).

Your interaction with each of these classes of middle-man – agents, wholesalers, logistics – will be different, and you will have to bear these differences in mind as you sell to your potential customers and as you attempt to strike up partnerships of varying intensity and of differing purposes.

And while you are doing this, please also remember that there are plenty of distributors who sell into specialised markets. Where do you think Chinese restaurants or Indian takeaways get their product – the rice, the spices and the rest? They are served by specialist wholesalers, and you will never reach them (that Chinese or Indian outlet, that is) unless you use the right channel. And, of course, that also goes for anybody else you sell to; it's pretty obvious, if you don't use the right channel, you won't get to the accounts that you want to.

Fish and chip shops, too, buy from specialist suppliers who have access to the small range, but quite large sales-per-store items that fish and chip shops use – oil, fish, potatoes. And you may be surprised to learn that they buy more potatoes than fish.

The largest players – contract caterers, fast-food outlets, some pub and restaurant chains – buy in such large quantities that they can persuade distributors to just – well – distribute without owning the goods and without adding a margin along the way. Instead, the customer in this case (the caterer or fast-food operator, for example) pays a fee for the logistics service irrespective of what is supplied and irrespective of its value – within reason the price per case is the same for frozen fries and gold bars.

And some products have specialist suppliers too. Produce, meat, and fish (at least in their short-life, fresh format) require specialist buying teams, specialised storage facilities, and specialised distribution vehicles. So it's not really a surprise that specialist distributors handle much of this type of product that finds its way into foodservice. I could go on, because there are many specialist distributors – either in terms of products that they sell or sectors they serve, or even both. But I won't. Nevertheless you should, indeed you must, take into account the route you use for the products you sell to the markets and customers you want to reach. And the reason is simply that if you haven't chosen, or don't use, the channels that are used by operators in the sectors that you want to sell to, your product just won't find its way to the customers you want to get it to.

●

Take care to ensure that your distribution channels are aligned with your target customers. *Using the inappropriate channel means no customer and that means no sale.*

Let the people rule

I had a boss many years ago, I'll call him Brian (primarily because that was his name). Brian taught me many useful things. When you sit in a meeting, make sure your back is to the window so that when the sun shines in, it doesn't blind you – but blinds him instead. And with your back to the window, you're likely to be facing the door; so when someone comes in you can see them straight away, but he has to turn round. You have the advantage.

Brian also taught me that the purpose of business is to be nice to people. Be nice to people and what will they do? They'll give you money

But what is 'nice'? A nice shiny car is nice; the nicer it is, the more money you'll want to pay for it. A haircut is nice; the nicer the haircut, the more you'll tip the hairdresser. What is nice about foodservice? Is it a shiny car – or a haircut? Is it a product or a service? The answer is, as we've seen, both product (principally food) and a service – but more of the latter.

You'll pay £8.95 for a steak in your local restaurant. You'll also pay ten times as much for steak at a restaurant in Bray with the name Blumenthal on the door. What's the difference between the steak for £8.95 and the steak for £89.50? The difference is in perception of 'niceness'. The ingredients may be three times nicer in Bray – the service is seven times nicer, adding up to a total of ten times nicer.

And again: you're in a restaurant, how much will you pay for a glass of water poured from a tap? Probably nothing. How much will the thirsty traveller in the middle of a desert pay for a glass of water poured from a tap? A small (or even a large) fortune. The glass of water is the same; what's different is the thirsty traveller's need. The customer's need state is an unsatisfied desire – and is the means by which operators can charge more.

Similarly, I hope you'll agree that we have established that foodservice has its own personality – and its personality is different from the personality of the retail sector. Order and structure in the retail world give way to entrepreneurism and seat of the pants in foodservice. Earlier I had characterised this foodservice world as chaotic, but that word hides a spectrum of issues which are important to you, a supplier or potential supplier, to the foodservice sector.

For starters, the people who inhabit foodservice understand what this chaos means. They are all cut from the same cloth. In character, they are friendly 'people people'. They are driven by their passion or joy in creating a suitably hospitable space for their customers. This is particularly noticable at the front, customer-facing parts of the business. And this area is, as we've already established, the significant and informative point of difference between foodservice and retail. The front-facing person, no matter whether he is a chief executive, manager, or a gig-economy operative, succeeds only when he or she is hospitable.

And because hospitality is the leitmotiv of the food-service character at the customer-facing interface, it therefore extends up the chain through various layers of management to the top, and across all parts of the food-service business – including crucially for you, the supplier – it spreads into the otherwise forbidding worlds of procurement and operations.

Why am I making such a meal of this? The answer is very simple: because you are selling to people whose character is about hospitality; that means that you must make sure your character is likewise driven by hospitality.

Let's work out what this means. As a supplier, your interaction with people in foodservice is broadly in the space that we can call 'selling' – your fundamental reason for interacting with foodservice is to sell something. Not necessarily – or actually not at all – in a hard-nosed way.

Like all good salespeople you will work out the character of the person you are dealing with and construct your story and employ the styles that will appeal most directly to your counterpart – the person or people you want to sell to.

Now we are getting close to the nub of the point I want to make which is simply this: you, and your salesman colleagues, must fit with the foodservice personality if you are to succeed.

And crucially, the factors that make you succeed in retail are not necessarily – I would argue they have nothing to do with – what makes you successful in foodservice. In retail, you have to play to the retailers' character of order and structure. Your salespeople will be ordered and structured.

To be successful in foodservice they will have to understand, mirror, and, ideally, adopt the hospitality personality. But please note that I am not arguing that your successful foodservice salespeople will lack order and structure – far from it – it's just that these attributes will merely support their hospitality mindset and will not be in front of it.

In a nutshell, your successful foodservice sales resource will match, as perfectly as possible, the personality of the foodservice sector.

Now, how often have you heard that being offered a position in the foodservice supply division of a manufacturing company is a suicide note for career development? Quite a few times, I would venture.

But it isn't the case. Often the motivation behind career development options, such as a move from retail selling to a commercial role in foodservice, are to do with the individual's (probably comparative) lack of sales success in retail. So, the management thinking goes, let's 'promote' this person to foodservice, and with a bit of luck the likely outcome will be that he, or she, will decide to move on.

But it needn't be like this. Check out the individual's skills as a person and see if the foodservice personality fits much better. You may find that the failed retail salesperson is a perfect shoo-in for a highly successful career in foodservice. This 'failed' retail salesperson may be just the person you are looking for to launch your business into foodservice or to reinvigorate your currently lacklustre foodservice business.

And if you were so bold as to try the following as an experiment, I'm prepared to bet that should you transfer your most successful retail people to foodservice, she would fail or, at best, perform with mediocrity in this hospitable business. The reason? The successful, retail-centric personality will not be right for foodservice.

So, it all boils down to horses for courses.

And, of course, this doesn't only apply to your salespeople, nor indeed only your foodservice-facing functions – customer relations, delivery, and the rest. It also applies to your internal team. They need to be chosen for their ability to interact empathetically with the foodservice market whether they are marketing people, brand managers, product managers, and the like, or finance and, dare I say especially, human resources. Their understanding of how the foodservice sector thinks and acts is vital if you are to recruit, train, and support your team.

So be sure to chose your foodservice team on the basis of its fit with the foodservice personality.

I have a problem retail salesperson. She doesn't seem to perform as well as I think she can. *Transfer her to foodservice sales and watch her shine.*

Appetite for apps

I am not 'appy with the title of this chapter. I had considered calling it something food-punning like 'Chips and chips' or 'Bytes and bites' but these technology-related terms are pretty old-fashioned now, so 'apps' it is.

I was having a meal with my daughter; my smartphone tingled in my pocket. I took it out and there was a simple question from a client that only required a few lines for a potentially swift reply. Before I got to the point of pressing send, my daughter said 'Let's get the etiquette right. No smartphones at the table'. Suitably abashed, I mumbled 'Sorry' and put my phone away. My enquirer would have to wait until the end of my meal – all of 60 minutes in the future – before I would be able to answer the question.

What's the point of this story? It's just to stress that eating out is a personal, person-to-person experience.

A point I've belaboured before is that people in the foodservice sector are people people and are not turned on by systems, processes, and technology. I'd guess that pretty much everyone in the sector has a smartphone and access to a computer and probably uses them for at least some part of their working life.

But all the available programmes and apps – email Twitter, Facebook, LinkedIn, Instagram, and more – while important to people in the sector as individuals are not generally drivers of their business. People in the sector want to deal with people and feelings, rather than technology.

This makes the industry a late adopter of technology – for instance, it was slow to embrace computers, and it takes much less interest in what computers can do than, say, the travel industry does. And all of this comes about because of the people-centric, hospitality-driven nature of the foodservice business.

Now, what does all this mean? Since the foodservice industry is about hospitality, human interaction is very important. It's all about feelings, and empathy, hunch and judgement. The type of person who is attracted to the sector is someone who is primarily driven by, and reacts to, feelings and certainly not by and to technology.

Let's look at the skills required in the kitchen for another insight into the non-technological nature of the foodservice sector. Cooks take food, which is shaped by nature and is therefore by definition not totally predict-able, and turn it into something that is as close to per-fection as possible. Of course, it all depends what you mean by perfection – the definition for a five-star chef is going to be different from that of a chef in a pub or a short-order operative in a burger joint. But the point is to take something that is variable and make it into some-thing that is perfect, however perfection is defined.

This process requires keen judgement: Is the sauce salty enough? Is the meat cooked yet? Is the Hollandaise sauce sufficiently homogenised?

And judgement is a human trait – not one shared by technology. What all this boils down to is the fact that people with their foibles and their instincts and their preferences are the essence of the foodservice sector. Those who thrive in this sector are the ones who are able to use their individual experience and judgment to achieve success. In other words, foodservice is human; it's not technical.

Therefore technology is not a driver for the sector – indeed it's a follower. There are, you won't be surprised to hear, exceptions to this – and we'll come to those shortly. But for now, since technology is a follower in foodservice, it's not surprising that the sector is a slow adopter of technology. Let's look at the history.

In the beginning, in the world of hospitality and food-service, technology was deployed in the back-of-house operation – it was, it still is, used for things like staff scheduling. It was also used for costing – and perhaps for storing recipes. It was the servant of the person working behind the scenes. Then along came point of sales systems – EPOS – that were initially used for taking payments and then expanded into analysing the information provided by the payment. Alongside EPOS were things like taking bookings and allocating tables.

And back in the kitchen, technology appeared in the form of coffee machines, microwaves, and combi ovens, etc., which provided ways of timing the required processes.

And then there is order placing. Gone are the days when the wholesaler's rep took the order or when orders were sent in by fax. Nowadays it's possible to place orders online, but despite that, telesales (and there you go with human interaction again) rule the roost, especially for smaller and independent operators, who are after all the majority in the foodservice sector.

So technology has found its way into foodservice, but primarily as the servant of the sector. So long as technology doesn't try to get ideas above its station – like taking over the business (or parts of it), so long as it doesn't try to provide too much information, and provided it doesn't get between the operator and his customers, technology is doing its job. The foodservice sector, as you don't need reminding, is driven by human interaction, and technology is the antithesis of that.

Thus, the sector is slow to move with the times. And please don't forget that when you develop some super, whizz-bang technology solution.

But wait. There are places where technology does take a starring role. Just think about rating apps (like TripAdvisor), ordering aggregators (like Just Eat and Deliveroo), and the plethora of other apps, whether generic (Groupon and Vouchercloud, for example), or apps that are created by individual operators, (Domino's website combined with its app is a prime example). And then don't forget that (almost) every restaurant, fast food, takeaway, and pub has its own website. And there are the many apps that offer to speed up internal systems, create communities of customers, and staff, help the customer rate the restaurant, make suggestions, get to the front of the queue, be the first to know about special offers – the list is large because many tech entrepreneurs have spotted many opportunities and operators are keen to engage with stakeholders – actual customers, potential customers, employees, suppliers – through technology.

In my view, the use of technology will only grow because of the expectations of consumers – especially millennials. It will build on the leading-edge technology that is being embraced by some operators, limited service food-to-go and fast food in particular. As I write, facial recognition software is now used in Hangzhou, China by the KPRO upmarket spinoff from KFC to simplify payment – just stare at the screen and the money is taken from your account.

And while we are talking about payment, one of the biggest issues that contributes to a negative view of a restaurant is the process of settling the bill. At the end of the meal, the customer wants to pay quickly and then leave. When this process is held up by first having to attract the waiter's attention, then receiving the bill, then checking it, then reconnecting with the waiter (where has he gone?), inserting the card in the machine, and waiting for several, or perhaps many, foot-tapping seconds while the slow internet connection takes its time. All of this can be stressful for the customer or at least adds an unpleasant note to what has been, hopefully, a pleasant meal. Technology can solve this problem in a variety of ways.

But even when it uses technology, the foodservice industry tends not to use the information that technology produces to make decisions. Why is this? I have several answers: first, the information is too bitty. It's a set of complications, it's a collection of disparate facts, and moreover this information is not brought conveniently into one place. Second, the information is difficult to access meaningfully. And third: as I think I may have mentioned (!) the sector is not in tune with technology – and that includes its minimal use of dashboards, spreadsheets, and ratings. It prefers the human touch.

So, while the industry is basically not enamoured with technology, it does have its place. Please take the time to work out if, and how, that place fits in with your operation and sales plans, now and into the future.

And be aware of the concept of a 'cohort'. This is the term used by sociologists to identify any group of people, typically defined by their age, who act in similar ways. The millennials are a cohort. They do things nowadays that are noteworthy and perhaps significantly different from any preceding cohort. For instance: they live on their smartphones; they are reportedly more self-oriented than their parents; and apparently prefer to buy experiences rather than things. The general expectation is that millennials will take these habits and thought processes with them as they grow older.

The likelihood is that they also will take their internet-centred approach with them as they age, and in doing so they will replace earlier cohorts with a different world-view. This means that use of and reliance on the internet and technology in general will become an even greater defining characteristic of the population in terms of how it works and behaves.

And what is the point of this delving into sociological issues? It's just that this new millennials cohort (and subsequent cohorts) will start to populate the foodservice sector, eventually becoming the people who run it. As the industry becomes filled with people who are completely familiar with technology, so the sector as a whole will become more technology-focused, more technology–aware, and more dependent on technology.

The millennials are being followed by an even more technology-oriented and knowledgeable cohort, already known by some as Gen Z, who over the next twenty or thirty years will again change the characteristics of the foodservice sector.

But despite all of these potential changes, in order to make foodservice work, it will still have be personable and hospitable and that means remaining people-focused.

Technology is advancing at unbelievable speed. *And because of the speed at which technology is evolving, the facts in this chapter will probably be out of date by the time you read this. But the sentiments and the insights will still be correct for a long time.*

Your factory – right or wrong

If you are in the manufacturing business, my betting is that one of the largest investments you have made in the last few years is the money you have spent on new equipment – maybe just a tweak to your production line or perhaps a completely new factory. And I'm pretty sure one of your overall considerations is ensuring efficiency, which is probably another word for profitability, at least in this investment context.

Your investment will, no doubt, have been justified on the basis of the number of hours the line can run without interruption, the speed at which it can process the unrefined inputs and turn them into packaged outputs, and the predictability of the required results. In other words, run lengths, speed, and predictability were the mood music, if not the primary objectives, of your investment. Your calculations will have taken each of these considerations (and more) into account and produced the specification for the equipment you've installed – possibly at great expense. Now, along comes foodservice and throws these assumptions into disarray. The reasons aren't hard to find but the solutions might be.

First, the reasons for the disarray. Let's start with the overall size of the foodservice opportunity for you and your products. It's likely to be one-ninth the size of the opportunity in the retail sector.

Now I realise we aren't talking as if you supply the full, complete needs of the retail sector, or the foodservice sector come to that. But as a first-level rule, your run lengths for foodservice customers will be one-ninth – that's 11% – of your normal or standard retail run length. Instead of running for a week to produce what the retail market requires, your line will run for just over half a day to satisfy your typical foodservice order.

And when it arrives, your foodservice order, in all probability, will be less standardised, more bespoke, then your retail products. This is because each operator will want something distinct from its competition. Remember, the foodservice operator is not a retailer trying to outdo the competition with prices or service levels and so offer better value from the similar product that is available from their competitors. Instead, remember that the foodservice operator is selling something that is unique to itself and that is not available from its competitors; and this means that your foodservice customers (in their ideal world anyway) will want products that are unique to them.

So, as a second factor, run lengths will be further reduced from the one-ninth of the retail equivalent to something much less in order to account for the unique requirements of your foodservice customers.

Their bespoke requirements will call for even shorter run lengths. The norm for foodservice products will be much shorter compared with typical run lengths for retail market products.

And then there is a third factor that determines efficiency, after run length and bespoke requirements – and that is predictability. Foodservice operators are less able to predict their needs than the typical retailer, because demand from foodservice operators is closely related to factors which affect their customers' buying behaviour – the weather, instantly changing fashion, television food programmes that generate immediate consumer interest (and therefore immediate demand), and sheer customer variability. So, predictability is not the name of the foodservice operator's game; and even if it were, as I've also pointed out, the information systems just aren't in place to make sufficiently accurate or helpful predictions.

So, on the grounds of run length, bespoke requirements and indifferent predictability, foodservice production demands will play havoc with the operation of your production line – and importantly, they will upturn you essential efficiencies and turn profit into loss.

Those are the considerations. But what can you do about them? Over the years, I have seen many apparent solutions, and they seem to have a distinctly zoological aspect!

Solutions include the 'ostrich' approach. Let's not look too far or too hard, and let's hope the problem will go away; and in the meantime, let's not run the line for the foodservice product.

Another solution is the 'tern' approach – take your turn. Carefully orchestrate the runs so that your foodservice run takes place at a time that minimises the lost time resulting from the need to clean and reset the line – perhaps delaying the foodservice run to the end of the week or to a convenient break in retail runs. The downside is that foodservice orders are delayed – maybe not a lot, but maybe significantly. The result though is often unhappy customers who are left waiting for their order to be delivered.

Or perhaps you adopt the 'squirrel' policy. You will produce stock and store it away (using expensive warehousing space), and await the call to order from the market. This adds to stockholding costs and runs the danger of building more than is ultimately needed with consequent costs in terms of wastage and disposal.

There are many more birds and animals that can be used to personify your approach but in the end one of the best solutions is to be the 'wise owl'. Be aware of the issues, measure them as best you can, use past experience to help shine a light on the future, but also plan for disruption in your production line. All the time, be aware of the special needs of the foodservice sector.

Demand from the foodservice sector is unpredictable and probably can never be predicted, so what can you do? Ultimately, the best practical solution is to have a line (or more than one?) dedicated to foodservice and give the people managing this line complete autonomy when it comes to run lengths and speed. This comes at a cost – not the least is the investment in the line – but it may be worth it.

Who decides?

Your product has taken its place on the plate in front of the diner who sits there in anticipation or maybe it's placed invitingly by the till in a coffee shop or at a caterer's checkout. Who decided it would be there?

It won't, by now I hope, surprise you to learn that the picture is complicated and unclear. In this chapter, I'm going to try to describe who decides what is on offer and how they interact with one another, and then use these insights to identify the implications for you, the supplier.

It all starts with the place – the place where the food is on offer. By that I mean what type of place, what type of outlet, is it? A high-end restaurant? A prison? A community pub?

Most places where you eat out have a bit of romance in the story of their creation (even schools and hospitals do), and the romance, that lingers (and may well be enhanced) as time goes by, tells you its story. And, in your reaction to the story lies the clue as to why you may end up eating there. Somebody, at some time, made the decision to open the place where you are going to eat. Maybe it was an individual or a couple of them or perhaps it was a large business or a committee or some amorphous group. This was the first step in the decision chain, because the type of business that was created influences the type of product you can provide.

So to begin to answer the question: What type of place is it that you're are supplying, let's start at the beginning with a story.Just outside Burford on the roundabout where the high street intersects the A40 near Oxford, there sits a restaurant, Giuseppe's Diner. What is its purpose? Why is it there? The classic answer is likely to be something like: to satisfy the customer's need or to provide something for the hungry traveller on their way from Oxford to Cheltenham.

But dig deeper, and you'll find another reason. Giuseppe didn't exist, but Joseph Robinson does, or did. He had a passion for cooking and wanted to show the world what he could do. So, Joseph brought Giuseppe's Diner into existsence because of his passion for food. But there might have been another reason. His father and uncle owned a car showroom on the roundabout, but competition, and the changing way that people bought cars, meant that they had to close down their showroom and find another use for their site. So, the purpose of Giuseppe's Diner could have been to provide rental income for Charlie and Eric Robinson. So in this simple story are just two of the many many reasons why any foodservice outlet exists

When the fundamental decision has been made as to what the place offers, there is an implementation phase – transferring plans into hard reality that determines the contents and layout of the kitchen, front-of-house design, the food receiving and storage area, the food serving area, and all the other areas. Each of these has to be planned, designed, costed, built, and brought into use. This is a long – and evolving – process. Along the way, compromises are made, details are incorporated, and decisions reached. These issues will influence the food that is going to be supplied; at this point, the people, whether influencers or deciders, are many – they can include the owner, the bank, financial backers, environmental health officers, other regulatory organisations, architects, kitchen designers, equipment providers, furniture designers, and many more.

Let's now assume that the operation is up and running. But nothing is fixed and final, because the operation will inevitably evolve over time. For example, crucial decisions must be made about the menu, which may continue to be altered depending on such factors as customer demand, ingredient pricing, and kitchen skills and availability. So menu construction is a core area where the decisions made will affect your prospects as a supplier. You'll want to find out who is involved in designing the menu – who decides what's on and what's off, how menu items are to be priced, what portion sizes are to be offered, and so much more.

Where are the decisions made? Are they made by the chef in the kitchen? By the chef alone? Or are others involved along the way? Who are they? Are they in the kitchen? Are they customers? Are they from head office?

If head office is concerned (and I use the term head office loosely because it can include things like the franchisor in a franchised operation), who is involved? Here is the beginning of a long list of job functions that may play a role: operations, finance, HR, health and safety, marketing.

And having made decisions, these decisions may be changed – perhaps in a planned way or perhaps in response to some external issue or maybe just because someone felt that change was needed. The decisions reached so far are then going to be changed by the interactions of all the people I've identified, and more.

So now let's assume that the fundamentals have been decided – what is going to be provided for the customer? Now the questions turn to who is going to provide it? This is where buyers are brought in with the job of deciding from whom and where to source the products that are needed. And buyers come in different flavours – they may be employed to buy within the business where they may be influential (influencing what is put on the customer's plate, for example) or they may be meek and mild and buy what they're told to buy or they may be part of an external procurement organisation or an individual purchasing consultant. And the key point for you to note is that yet more people are involved.

Now, what about the customer? While it is usual now to claim that the customer is the core and focus of everything that the operator does, the customer cannot make any decisions until options are put in front of him or her.

That is why I have first listed the people and the roles that influence what is going to be on offer. Of course, along the way, the decision-makers will have taken account of what the customer wants (maybe they have done some research) or what they perceive the customer wants (it's here that gut feel and experience are the guiding lights). But at this point, the customer is used as a point of principle, a benchmark, a theoretical entity – customers are not actually choosing or deciding anything yet. But when the doors open and the menu is placed in front of the diner, that's when the actual decisions are made by the customer.

So let's open the doors and let the customers in. This is the moment of truth where their choices become all-important. But, even before this, the customer has made a choice, that is, deciding where to eat. The customer has to choose 'where' before 'what'. And this decision is often a shared decision. A party of people, whether a couple on a date or executives at a business lunch or an office Christmas party, make a joint decision, trying to take into account the needs and preferences of the people in the party. Perhaps wheelchair access is needed or a strict vegetarian or vegan is in the party. Or maybe one person in the party has recently overdosed on pizza and is looking for a change.

But let's assume that the place has been chosen and the customers are sitting there. They know they are going to order something but what? Perhaps this is a regular haunt and the decision is always the same. Or maybe there has been a recommendation from a friend or a website or an article in the newspapers.

There may be a chalkboard with dishes of the day or perhaps the A-board on the pavement outside has raised interest. And then, at last, there's the menu. This has been constructed with a bit of skill, a bit of craft and experience, plus the exigencies of design. Is there enough room to include all the descriptions of available dishes? Is there sufficient space for highlighting the signature dish? How to accommodate specials?

And then the choosing begins. The party may influence each other – or individuals may remain true to their own preferences and selections. Perhaps the waiter has been asked for his suggestion or even recommendation. In the final analysis, customers' choices reflect a measure of emotion with a pinch of preference and experience, and a dollop of ecommendation. Price can come into it too – although often not openly acknowledged.

One way and another, our diner or pub or restaurant faces a barrage of customer choices that are not always predictable. So, choosing what products to offer and serve is complicated for the foodservice operator, and the outcome is uncertain.

And this is where you as a supplier of food, say, to the wide retail market, can play a role. You can make available your experience and your researched insights into consumer preferences. You are well placed to suggest ways to save the operator's costs – by reducing wastage, by assisting with portion control and suggesting ways to play tunes on portion sizes. You can suggest ways to improve efficiency in the back-of-house operation where the products and categories that you supply are of concern. Maybe you have ideas, and more importantly, you may have evidence about trends that your customer should know about.

And you can suggest ways to increase demand – perhaps you have insights gained from your retail expertise on how to describe a product on the menu in such a way that it will inspire customers to order or to order more frequently

I supply lots of products to the retail sector. How can I help the foodservice operator? *Operators are hungry (pun partially intended) for your ideas to increase demand – and reduce costs. You have experience and insights gained from the retail market. So use them.*

If it's not this, it's that

We've looked at the foibles of the foodservice sector, especially those that make it different from retail. And along the way, we've discovered sectors – restaurants, pubs, workplace, universities, and the list goes on. In total, as I've already said, I divide the eating-out market into approximately 100 sectors and subsectors. And then there are many ways of looking at just one subsector – you may want to include something called managed and tenanted pubs, and you may want to split the category into two or even more.

So, there are many ways to define what we are talking about when we want to describe the individual elements of the market.

I have inevitably been using words which are recognisable and easy to understand. We all know a school when we see one or a hospital or a roadside kiosk. Or we think we do. But do we? A pub is a pub isn't it? Well, not necessarily – does that establishment possess the attributes of pubness that meets our definition?

As well as defining on the basis of type of venue, you can define the market in other ways too. For instance, you can define an outlet by size: how many meals does it serve? Or what is its floor area? Both of these define how a business operates – and can therefore be usefully employed as a way of discriminating between types of businesses you want to go for, and those you don't.

You can base your analyses of different types of food-service businesses or outlets on the types of meals they serve or the times of day their menu usually is designed for. If you sell bacon or toasters, then concentrating on those outlets (or businesses) that make a feature of breakfast or sell a lot of breakfasts is a shrewd way to target your market. (By the way, they may or may not offer these breakfasts only at what we call breakfast time, generally taken to be before 10:00 or 10:30 in the morning.)

You may want to define the market by geography – by county or postcode perhaps. Or by the type of location – rural, seaside, city centre, and so on.

And another useful defining characteristic is whether the operation makes its own purchase decisions – or whether these are made somewhere else, say, at a head office. The natural split is between chain (or group) oper-ations and the independents. And perhaps there is a third type of group operator called undisciplined where the decision making is not strictly controlled by formal rules or where there are such wide parameters that management at individual locations can make decisions within the choices or options provided by head office.

The list of defining characteristics is much longer than this. In my early days in the foodservice sector, one of the leading clients for information was Dulux, the paint people. Why? Because foodservice outlets need refurbishing every few years, and refurbishment means painting (amongst other things). Dulux, or its owner ICI, commissioned surveys that measured the numbers of windows each outlet had and defined the market accordingly – a ten-window establishment, a twenty-window establishment. and so on.

The difficulty with any and all of these approaches is that they are more complex than simply defining the operation by what it does. So, if it serves meals, usually with the option of having alcohol, let's call it a restaurant; if it serves food to the under-elevens, let's call it a primary school; if it has lots of bedrooms and puts up guests who pay, let's call it a hotel (perhaps with more than 200 bedrooms); or if they don't pay and are forced to spend the night there, it's going to be a prison – although if they're not well, it's more likely to be a hospital; and so on.

This approach to dividing the sector is customer-centric because, after all, it's how customers view their eating-out options. And this approach is also useful, because it is usually possible to identify what category any outlet falls into, just by looking at it.

In the end, these function-based definitions work best both as a means of having a common language and a declared common basis for discussion, and as a way of classifying types of outlet – and classification provides clarity.

And in the end, in my experience, the other ways of defining the sector (by size, day part, etc.) fail because they are difficult to assign to any specific establishment –

how do you know how many breakfasts, lunches, and dinners an outlet sells just by looking at it? Nevertheless, these factors can be useful ways of discriminating between different classes of outlet. So, what's the solution? It's probably to combine the factor you find most helpful with a broader function-based definition – a chain-owned pub or a hotel that serves food at lots of conferences and so on.

The lesson then is to be clear about classifications and to use more than one for each outlet so that you can slice and dice the market in ways that provide meaningful chunks which can be examined and sold to explicitly.

It's also important to ensure that we use classifications correctly when communicating with others – if what I call a gastropub turns out to be what you call a pub restaurant then as our conversation develops and we start to formulate plans, our thoughts, analyses, insights, and conclusions will go awry. So, define clearly and accurately – and use the terms conscientiously.

Let's look again at some additional ways of defining foodservice.

A very helpful way to categorise the sector is to look at how important food is within the overall business of the outlet. We can do this by getting the answers to some simple questions like: Is serving food a fundamental part of its reason for existing? Or does it exist to do something else – and does it only provide food on the way? Using this approach, I think there are three major market segments.

The first consists of outlets that exist to serve food – and in this category, I will place restaurants – both full service and quick service. And I'll also include pubs which arguably exist to serve drinks as their prime purpose. But food is such an important component of this sector nowadays, I think it's possible to safely include it alongside restaurants.

Another type of outlet that exists to serve food comes up hard against the fundamental theme in this book that the personality of foodservice is different from retail. But it's not always true! It doesn't apply to some parts of the foodservice sector which, on examination, share many similarities with retail – and herein lies a topic that many people comment on and that I've mentioned before – the blurring between foodservice and retail. In this space we should include places that serve food to go places and these places share many characteristics with convenience stores and petrol stations. They all serve packaged sandwiches, savoury snacks and cold drinks for the customer to eat right away. The next segment includes outlets, like hotels, that provide a service that customers pay for, and through habit and long-standing practice or because it's a sensible thing to do, they provide food as well. An important part of what defines this segment is that it provides a service that customers pay for – and so, in addition to hotels (and other places that provide overnight accommodation like B&Bs or caravan parks or holiday camps), we can include places where people go to participate in sport or other leisure activities, or go as spectators. There are a multitude of sub-sectors here – cinemas, golf clubs, race tracks, theme parks, football clubs, and zoos. And many more.

In each place, whether offering overnight accommodation or providing some leisure-based activity, the main purpose is not to provide food. Food is there as an add-on that keeps the visitor on site. Foodservice is not the major part, it may not even be a minor part of the offer, but it exists nevertheless. And because it's not a core part of the offer, it is often not done well or it's done grudgingly, perhaps with minimal investment.

The final way to segment the foodservice market using this typology, is to include outlets where customers don't pay for the service (or don't pay fully for it) as in the previous category, but where food is provided because their customers need it. In this segment we can include schools, hospitals, prisons, and many other types of institutions, such as care homes, universities, and the military. Here, too, food is not supplied as the core part of the service provided but must be provided nevertheless.

And in this category, I will also include workplace feeding, often referred to as B&I –business and industry – although it also includes workplace feeding for people involved in non-business activities. For example: doctors, nurses, administrative staff in hospitals; or employees of local and national government; or people working for charities.

This third category is characterised by providing food that is (often, but not always) subsidised in some way. And this has major implications for attitudes towards costs – they must always be kept low.

Using this typology, we have identified three major categories: outlets that exist to serve food, outlets that provide a price-based service where food has to be provided in addition to the service, and outlets that exist to provide another service and where subsidised food is provided.

This is a clear and hopefully simple structure for you to get your mind round. The only problem is that it is too simplistic.

●

What's in a name? *If you can name it, you have the option of selling to it. If you don't put a name to it, you'll miss lots of tricks.*

There is no information

This chapter has gained its title from the fact that I often jokingly tell people that I make my income by charging £1 every time someone tells me there is no information about the foodservice sector.

There is information, but what its nature is and where you'll find it is difficult for people from the retail market to understand.

What do people mean when they say that there is no information about foodservice? They have put on their retail hat and look for the type of information that sustains them day in and day out when dealing with multiple retailers. It's the detailed lines of sales data, analysed by SKU, store location, even day of the week and time of day. Acres of data that need teams of specialists armed with data visualisation tools, or increasingly, artificial intelligence algorithms to make sense of. It is the type of information supplied by data collection and analysis firms like IRI and Kantar.

Because this data is available, is so detailed, and is supplied in more or less real time, every company active in the sector is expected to use it. And that means a lot of companies invest a lot of financial resources in acquiring (and then analysing) the data. And because so much money has been devoted to the data, there is plenty more money available for collecting even more data, refining it, and presenting it in ever more meaningful, indeed colourful and innovatively creative, ways.

It is possible to do this because the food market (and drink, toiletries, and related markets) ease the data collection process by coding their products and because retailers collect information at their tills or on their online sites, for every single transaction they carry out.

Thus, a vast data industry has been brought into existence that does many things. From your point of view as a supplier to the retail sector, it is used to estimate the size of markets, measure market share, track trends over time, identify who buys the products, establish the impact of special pricing and promotional activities, and much more. And you use this information for your own purposes – to help confirm whether a proposed investment is likely to pay off and how quickly; you use it to provide the context for your strategy or your annual budget. And you also use it in discussions and negotiations with your retail customers to underpin your proposition, to demonstrate your knowledge, and to make use of language based on data that is common to you and your customer so that you both speak from the same page.

And, probably not surprisingly, you want to do the same in the foodservice sector. In this, you are encouraged by some of your foodservice customers who claim to want the same sort of information – but probably don't really need it unless they are in one or two special businesses like distribution or contract catering.

But let's stop here and start to listen to what the food-service sector is trying to tell you.

Foodservice is telling you that at heart it is a different business to retail – and a business that you have to take on its terms. Its purpose in life is not, primarily, to provide food and drink, but to provide a service based on hospitality. It is telling you that it goes about its business by being hospitable and personable – and not by being driven by data.

So: stop and rethink the question of data from the foodservice angle.

It is actually incorrect that there is no information. There is information; there is lots of it. The key is that, as the military say, it's hidden in plain sight. By this I mean, it's there, obvious to all but not visible unless you shift your mind a bit.

In the case of retail, information generally means numbers, which may be used to construct hypotheses, plans, and route maps that describe how to proceed. In foodservice, hospitality is what is used to help construct hypotheses, plans, and route maps.

Hospitality is not numbers, it is action. That means when you look for information in foodservice, you should be looking out for what is happening and not forever looking for the numbers.

Observe what people do, how things are changing, listen to what people tell you about why things are changing, how they have developed and where they are likely to go. Look out for the little things that may be the sign of big things to come. The Seattle Coffee Company was founded in the UK by Ally and Scot Svenson in 1995. It was a small business, that the founders deliberately based on a fairly unknown (in the UK at any rate) US company known as Starbucks. The Seattle Coffee Company thrived, and when it reached the grand total of 18 stores in 1997, Starbucks stepped in and, acquiring the business as a platform for growth, used it to to launch an onslaught on the British consumer. Would you have been able to identify where the Seattle Coffee Company would have ended up? How many other Seattle Coffee Companys are there right now?

You can acquire an informed opinion by talking to people – operators and their suppliers – read the media, find out what Twitter is saying. And you should talk to family and friends and the man in the pub. The more you talk the more you'll learn.

At the same time, you can gain specific knowledge about the accounts you are selling to – especially, but not exclusively, if they are active on the high street. And if they aren't on the high street (maybe they are a contract caterer), try to find ways to taste their offer – get yourself invited to a staff cafeteria run by the caterer.

You can certainly find out about high street offers in the simplest, and most enjoyable way, by visiting their outlets and buying a meal – or having a coffee. I suggest you make it a rule never to visit a foodservice account without having recently eaten at one (or more) of their stores.

When you pay a visit like this, what should you do? Observe. Gain a feel for the operation, and you can share your opinions and insights with your contact when you next sell to him or her. Remember, people in the foodservice sector want you to share in what they offer people – and by demonstrating that you have taken this implied sharing to heart, they will welcome you and take you seriously.

What should you be observing? Look at the outlet from the view of the customer – is it clean? And does it look welcoming? Are you welcomed by the serving staff? Are they organised? Or clearly under pressure? Are they helpful – and engaged with the brand? Look at the other diners – who are they? Families with kids? Singles? Millennials? Business people? What does this tell you about the business compared with its competitors? I haven't told you to visit their sites as well – but of course, you will.

And since the business is about service – more than food, focus on the service first and only then on the food. And remember, numbers do not drive this sector.

However, with a career of over 30 years spent in measuring the foodservice sector, I am not blind to the need for numbers in the sector. One of my mottoes, as a former scientist, is 'if you can't measure it, it doesn't exist'. Numbers in foodservice are important when they are used for context and justification, but they are less useful when they are used to fix things to a decimal point or to measure what is happening on a day by day, week by week, or even month by month, basis. Foodservice just doesn't work like that.

Because foodservice doesn't much care for numbers, it doesn't take special efforts to generate them – or use them. It doesn't have large, integrated systems that stretch back and forth up and down the supply chain.

It is happy to place its daily orders for food, for example, by telephone even though online options are available. When foodservice people meet, they don't exchange numbers, but they do exchange ideas, gossip, and insights.

So information in foodservice is fundamentally different to information in retail – and as a supplier my advice to you is to take the foodservice sector on its own terms.

This will require a different mindset from you – and your colleagues. It will require different reporting processes – the monthly or quarterly figures you supply about your foodservice business to the board or to headquarters will be estimates (not hard facts) and should be understood as such.

But there are important exceptions. As we now know, foodservice is large and sprawling, and while whole segments of it do not run on data, some segments are closer to retail and do. For example, distributors – they are more akin to retailers in their mindset and operations than the customers they serve. Distributors handle thousands of SKUs; they have categories to manage; they may be brand-focused or they may have an impressive own-label portfolio; they sell large quantities of their main categories; they have many many suppliers who fight hard for their business; they have high levels of bargaining power which they are prepared to wield; they use their suppliers to provide them with information and guidance on many matters – for no charge; they are in a very competitive space, including large, mid-sized, and very small, street-fighting companies; they have to be utterly efficient; the largest ones have many sites across which to operate; they make major investments in handling real-time information. For all these reasons, they are attuned to information as data and numbers – and will expect you, as a supplier, to respect that and meet their requirement for information.

Contract caterers, as I have already noted, are different from distributors, but they share many of their characteristics. They also look for data and numbers – and not least because in some respects they act as retailers – just think about the confectionery and snack products they sell at the checkout tills at many of their outlets.

Fast-food operators, with franchisees as well as customers to keep happy, also need data. But they generate much of it themselves from their sophisticated electronic till systems.

These are some exceptions to the general rule that foodservice lives on things and activities not data and numbers. So must you.

Why can't I find the numbers for foodservice that I need?
Do you really need them in the way you envisage? The world of foodservice uses numbers only as part of its equation for success. Knowing 'things' is a crucial requirementt for foodservice operators.

Consumer information?
Trade information?

There has been a revolution in the last ten years in the way that food manufacturers approach the foodservice sector. Nowadays forward-thinking companies make real efforts to understand the ultimate consumer, in other words their customers' customers.

They have done this because adopting a consumer-focussed strategy offers them a number of advantages. In the foodservice sector, two are particularly crucial.

The first is that by understanding the final consumer, your product development, sales, and marketing activities can be based on what is most likely to succeed, And second, a real understanding of the operators' customers, as well as sharing your knowledge and insights, means that you become a genuine partner with the operator.

The consumer is the same consumer whether she is buying from a shop or a foodservice outlet. Thus, the understanding and processes that you can bring to bear in consumer-facing foodservice strategies are generally driven by well-established strategies that you already deploy in the retail sector, and I assume you already deploy them with some success.

This approach particularly benefits the suppliers of products, such as soft drinks, snacks, and confectionery, that are sold through the foodservice channel as if it were another retail channel. Within foodservice, suppliers of these products, generally considered to be impulse purchases, make exceptional use of the insights they have gained from their fully focussed retail experience.

Additionally, suppliers who monitor the consumer are able to create products for use in the foodservice operators' kitchens that will please the consumer's taste buds! With this knowledge it is then often a small step to creating new products and promotional packages that appeal to foodservice operators.

In other words, leading foodservice suppliers bring as much consumer knowledge to bear on their activities as their retail colleagues do. And with this knowledge they are able to create and present food offers that appeal to both consumer and operator. If you don't do this already or if you hadn't thought of it, you should consider emulating them.

But the retail-based consumer information model can only be stretched so far in foodservice because the sector differs from retail in two fundamental ways.

For a start, distributors control the routes to market for many sectors and operators. And second, operators do not generally stock a range of products and brands – they stock a single product that is right for their customers and their own needs.

This means that you can't solely rely on a customer-facing strategy – you also have to incorporate it into an overall structure that takes full account of these two trade-related factors. Trade information is therefore fundamental to your success in the foodservice sector – and, I would further argue, that access to, and then deploying, trade information is a more significant success factor than it is in the retail sector

For instance, compared with retail, the foodservice sector is much more complex and fragmented. It is a highly entrepreneurial market where operators are much more likely to make seat-of–the-pants decisions than retailers would ever do. And the caterer is: part housewife, part manufacturer, part retailer. Products and messages must be carefully tailored to meet these triple needs.

In addition, the fundamentally important role of the distributor within the foodservice system means that you will have to create the products, ranges, and prices that appeal to them. Understanding the consumer has a role to play in this process but so does a proper understanding of the foodservice operator. At the same time, you should understand the requirements of each of the different distribution channels – broadline delivered, cash and carries, product specialist wholesalers etc. – and the different sectors they service.

In my experience, successful consumer-facing foodservice suppliers also have a well-honed trade-facing approach which recognises the complexities of the market and the consequent balance between fragmented market needs and the resources that they are able to deploy to satisfy them.

Again in my experience, successful foodservice suppliers, also track the myriad continuing changes in the market and constantly re-evaluate the resulting opportunities and priorities that arise from these changes. Successful suppliers also have strategies in place which recognise the differing – and often conflicting – needs of the consumer, the operator, and the distributor.

Persuading the operator to use a specific product is only part of your battle – persuading the distributor to stock it is the other part.

And finally, foodservice distributors use their own sales data which provides a comprehensive and very detailed picture of their market – and one that accurately reflects changes over time – but which, I must acknowledge does not give a complete picture of the market as a whole!

Nevertheless, manufacturers with pockets deep enough to gain access to this information see the same basic data as do their distributor customers – and they can therefore identify the trends and characteristics that are, or should be, identified by the distributor. At least you can start from the same page.

When I have a choice of information, where should I put my money? Follow some of the successful consumer-focused suppliers and also have a well thought out, structured, and on-going approach to all significant trade issues – at the level of both the operator and the distributor.

A happy medium

The importance of the subject of this chapter probably won't come as a surprise given what we have discovered about the foodservice sector. It concerns the topic of communication – and especially communication between you, the supplier of products that foodservice operators use, and the foodservice operator himself or herself.

Let's recall some things we have already discussed. The sector is diffuse, its channels are complex, and decisions are often made in a chaotic manner. But you, if a habitué of the retail supply chain, are used to communication with a user (aka the consumer) who is all around, who is capable of being characterised in a relatively small number of meaningful and helpful ways, and whose decision making, while not always rational, is at least understandable.

Further, communicating with the retail consumer is (or at least it was until the relatively recent advent of social media, search engines, and online advertising) a fairly straightforward process: decide a message, confirm the medium, press the button – and wait, with bated breath, for the money to roll in.

We can be sure that advertising on television works as the process is known and the reach is fairly predictable. Similarly advertising on radio or in the press, whether it is daily or weekly, is effective. And so is outdoor advertising and many of the alternative media that our creative world has generated.

While the newer electronic world is less certain, it still provides channels of communication that are fairly predictable and that, to some degree, can be almost guaranteed to reach the desired audience.

And what ties these channels together is their reach – generally large or at least reasonable – and their predictability: you have a reasonable idea of who will see, hear, or experience your message. What is more, when the message is received by the consumer, there is at least some chance that he or she will have the time (perhaps only measured in a few seconds) to recognise the message and absorb something of what it says. Of course, none of this guarantees that the receiver of the message will do anything as a result of receiving it – but you can always hope.

Now let us consider these features in the context of the foodservice market. This market, you won't need reminding is quite small – perhaps a few hundred thousand buying points compared with sixty million consumers (although that does include the under-fives who might pester but don't pay!).

Foodservice is also structured in many different ways – in other words, many 'demographics' are at play – pubs and police stations, coffee shops and cafeterias, hospitals and hotels, and, and, and... Consumers, by contrast, are much easier to classify.

As a consequence, and mirroring this structure, the media used to reach decision makers in foodservice are fragmented and generally small scale. Although your potential foodservice customers – chefs, purchasing managers, ops people, etc. – read and see the main media, there are not enough of them to make it financially justifiable to use television or the national press or other mass media to get your foodservice message out to them.

Nevertheless, in the past, suppliers have used television advertising to reach decision-makers in restaurants and pubs. Alveston Kitchens, manufacturers of cheesecakes and other frozen desserts, created and aired advertisements on TV in the 1980s. But the fact that they didn't repeat the exercise, and their competitors did not take up the challenge, probably indicates the lack of success of this initiative.

Returning to my main focus, foodservice people are gregarious; they like trying other people's foodservice ideas – usually in the expectation that they'll learn something of value and something that they can use or modify and then recycle in their own kitchen or in their front-of-house activities.

How information flows through the foodservice sector gives us some clues about how to communicate with this diverse and complex business.

So, you should be saying: Well, here is how it goes. Don't think about mass media – your message is likely to be directed at a few thousand people, maybe fewer. But do think about fractured media, trade media, trade marketing (using the supply chain to spread your message for example), networking, and trade shows. Plus, as you can imagine, there are growing opportunities in the social media space.

Let's summarise these media, and note that the resources, not to say the skills, needed to get your message to the foodservice sector are different from successful mass communications with customers in the retail space.

Suppliers have, for many years, used magazines to get their message to their customers in the foodservice sector. And that is true even today when, so we are told, magazines are dead. Well they aren't. There is a wide choice, and nowadays they are often very focused on a small sector – garden centres or boutique hotels, covering specific categories – kitchen equipment and frozen food.

But not only magazines. Trade shows have always played a part in the foodservice sector – and they work because, and again I'll say it, the sector is driven by meeting people and sharing ideas. Trade shows are good for that. And a plethora of choices exist – perhaps too many. They are usually quite specific, covering pubs or takeaways, lunch time or casual dining. Their visitor base is likewise focused.

For you as a supplier to utilise this targeted and fragmented media demands some basic skills, the same ones required in most marketing endeavours. They include identifying the market, having a clear, appropriate, and effective message, and all the rest of the communications toolkit.

These skills will apply in foodservice just as much as they do in retail consumer communications. But how they are applied is different. When using your retail communications skills and when applying your strategy to foodservice, please stop, and look both ways before crossing, because the traffic may be going in an unexpected direction. As in so many things, foodservice is different from retail.

What is the fundamental purpose of communicating to foodservice operators? *It's to keep in touch and to open the door for further discussions. Today's email generation of foodservice decision-makers, is being replaced in the workplace with the Facebook generation. Before long, their cohort will be replaced with the Snap generation. Messages and media will have to evolve.*

Experience and expectations

One of the results of the structural issues in the food-service sector is the scale of the decisions made here. In other words, at least compared with the retail sector, foodservice moves incrementally rather than in large strides.

This comes about for a number of reasons. First is the relatively small size of the players in the market. The very largest – at least in the UK – is McDonald's, followed fairly closely by Mitchells & Butlers. Both of these companies have UK sales of about £2 billion. In most people's books this is a pretty large amount, but compared with the behemoths in retail, say Tesco or Asda with annual sales in the order of tens of billions of £s, it is fairly small.

Small scale immediately leads to small(er) decisions in terms of the values and volumes that are involved. And this, in turn, means that foodservice sales move in (comparatively) small steps rather than large strides.

Second, foodservice is flexible, and decisions in the sector can often be put off to a later date, assuming that flexibility in the system will iron out any issues along the way.

So, decisions are not only based on smaller values than in retail, they are also often made later in the day. The foodservice sector moves to different rhythms compared with retail. Decisions need to be based on different assumptions, timescales need to be adjusted, and a host of variables must be modified if you are to be successful.

That's not to say that many of the fundamentals that make the world go round don't apply to foodservice. It's still a place where a well-honed argument is likely to win the day; it's a place where the imperative to make a profit still reigns; foodservice responds positively to helpful suggestions; and in most ways, it is the same as any other market, including retail.

And yet: the way that the market is viewed in your company, if it is typical of companies that supply the retail sector with only limited involvement in foodservice, will focus on the retail way of doing things.

Your colleagues at a senior level will probably have had a career in retail (as may you). This experience will be reflected in how they view business in the sector. They will understand arguments that are set out by their colleagues to explain the need for a change of pack design or pricing; they will be receptive to arguments about special deals for major customers, knowing how they are likely to respond. It also means that the way forecasting is done in your retail business, and the assumptions that underpin it, will be governed by the experience – not merely the expectations – of your senior colleagues in the retail sector.

But when it comes to foodservice? Well, they will have heard that it's growing, and that it is more profitable than retail. Those may be their starting expectations even though, as we have seen they are not necessarily true.

They will have heard that foodservice is complex – but they may not appreciate what that complexity means. But you and I have investigated many of these complexities to show their nature and their relevance for you and your business. So, between us, we probably understand the foodservice better than your colleagues whose experience doesn't extend into foodservice.

Your colleagues may not appreciate that when you talk about major accounts in foodservice, their purchases pale in comparison with major retail accounts.

However it is important to realise that, because of their limited range, some foodservice operators spend exceptionally large budgets on their core products, fries, burger patties, buns, and so on as in the case of McDonald's. So note that this makes large, limited-range accounts especially alluring if you have the right categories in your portfolio.

Nevertheless, your colleagues may not be attuned to the overall speed (or lack of it) of decision making in foodservice. They may not understand the reasons for its slower growth, and when they listen to you talking about things like the slow rate of decision making or fragmentation in product specifications or the complexity of the market or the resources needed to land an order, they may think you are indulging in special pleading (which you are are) as an excuse for covering up some flaw (which you are not) – it's merely the way of the world in foodservice.

In short, your colleagues' expectations of the size of the opportunity and the rate at which you are able to gain significant size are just that: expectations. You have a job to do to translate expectations into reality, and sometimes you may wish that you were dealing with colleagues who have the same hard-won experience in the foodservice sector that you possess. That would make your job much easier.

Hope over experience? *You have experience of the food-service sector. Unfortunately most of your colleagues only have expectations. Make sure you keep impressing on them why your experience trumps their expectations.*

Where is the future?

Now, where do you go for ideas about the future? I'm talking specifically about new ideas about where the eating-out market is going and where the new ideas for tomorrow will be found. And that's the main point of this chapter. But while we're on the subject of the future, we'll also take a look at how to find ideas about new products – for both back and front of houe.

But let's start off with the big ideas for the future – what are the new formats and cuisines that will drive the foodservice sector forward over the next few years?

If you were to ask yourself this question for the retail sector, I'd guess you'd look at what the industry behemoths are doing and saying – and you'd probably have discussions with them. You may look at what they're doing at the moment, but once it's 'in store' so to speak, it's no longer the future, it's the here and now.You may look at what's happening in other countries as well. But I'd be pretty certain that you won't look at what's happening in the independent, corner shop segement of the UK market. It's not known for the innovation and sparkling ideas that will set the world of food retail alight in the years to come.

And that is a big difference compared to the world of restaurants. The big players do what they do – they are not able to change their spots. A pizza chain cannot reinvent itself as a on-trend purveyor of genuine Caribbean food and ambience. The normal way for these big players to develop a new idea is to create a new brand. That normally means developing a trial concept in one or two sites and see what the customers think – it's really just an expensive market research play. Or the large chain will acquire a smaller, emerging brand of a handful of units that seems to be going places or which the management of the larger brand think may represent the future.

And this holds the clue to where the future lies – and the answer to the question with which I kicked off this chapter. The place to look for the big ideas for the future is amongst the small players – the innovative entrepreneurs who have seen something that works elsewhere; or they think they have found a niche; or some idea has sparked their interest; or they have an investment in something else that they think can be extended into the restaurant space.

A major source of new ideas is the burgeoning street-food market. This is a relative newcomer to the eating-out sector and takes its inspiration from countries in the Far East where eating in the streets is how people consume food (and, an as an aside, it's how Londoners consumed food in the twelfth century!). Another source of inspiration has been the growth of food trucks in the

USA. The street-food wave has expanded rapidly in the UK and who knows whether it will last. It started off spontaneously with entrepeneurs with ideas and little cash – and a need to prove their idea. More recently, the street-food idea has been corralled and tamed with the emergence of specially located and resourced sites for street-food operators. But that is an aside because, the actual opertaors have a multitide of ideas that they try out and consumers vote with their wallets. Failure rates are high – or in reality they are not failures but just great ideas that failed to get traction. It's dynamic!

That means it's a place you should go to to see the future – the smaller players lead the way in foodservice, like they just don't in retail. And that's the main lesson from this chapter. But while we're discussing the future and big ideas, you will probably be asking yourself, why bother? Why can't you wait until the future arrives and then see what you can do to make some money out of it. Well, of course, that is a perfectly acceptable strategy – it's less risky than a bet on the future, but it reduces your opportunity to benefit from a correct bet.

It seems to me that the reason for you as a supplier to look out for the future big idea is that operators will regard you as forward thinking, and therefore they will see you as a good business to work with. Additionally, you will be in a great position to make suggestions to operators, and you will be well placed to come up with the products and services that the future will need.

And big ideas are not only about what operators will be doing. Big ideas for the supplier can be about the format of the product. In the kitchen it may be a choice between a powder or a paste or a liquid in a bottle, or it may be a choice between a frozen product, one delivered chilled or at an ambient temperature. Or the big idea may be concerned with the packaging – a pouch or a bottle or a can, or a choice of pack size – 25g or 5 kilos – that addresses an operator's back-of-house problems.

The operator will expect you, as the supplier, to come up with the solutions – and ideally you will identify the problem before the operator realises it is a problem. To be effective in this endeavour you will have to do many things. You will have to be in touch with operators – talking to them about their issues. You will look at other market segments (what are restaurants doing that can benefit contract caterers). You will be looking in other countries, not only in Europe and the USA, but the Far East, Australia, and South America. And you will also look at the retail market that you may know very well indeed. But, be careful of not falling into the trap of assuming that foodservice will just accept your retail product repackaged – and if you think that is the way to go, may I suggest that you re-read this book!

Where is the future? *In foodservice it's to be found in the undergrowth represented by the small entrepreneurial player – once the larger players have adopted an idea, it's no longer the future.*

Should you give up?

You are getting near to the end of this book and I hope that you have concluded that foodservice is for you even if you'll have to change your expectations, or your ways of working, or the people you employ. Maybe you'll have to make some big changes or, hopefully, just a few tweaks in key areas will be enough to set you on a successful road into foodservice. That's my hope.

But what happens when you have read this book, considered what it says for your business, and have decided that there are too many things that are just not right. And as a result, you have come to the conclusion that the foodservice sector is just not for you.

Is that the end of the road? Well, it may be. Perhaps the best thing to do is to give up any ideas about investing in a foodservice business and to stick to what you know, pursuing other potential areas. If that is your decision, then may I offer a piece of advice? Don't keep harking back to the foodservice sector. You have looked at it and decided it's not for you. So, don't waste any more time on it. At least for now. It's OK to come back to it in say a couple of years when your business may have changed and perhaps becomes more aligned with the demands of foodservice. Or perhaps your market has changed, and you really must see about changing your company so that it is better structured to adapt to the demands of foodservice. Or maybe something else has changed.

So, saying "no" now doesn't mean "no" forever– but it should (I would say, it must) mean that whenever anybody in your company raises the question: "Shouldn't we look at foodservice?" the answer for the next couple of years at least is "we've looked at it and it's not for us".

But there are other options to consider. And I will put a couple to you. The first is the Chinese Wall option.

You will have concluded from this book, I hope, that the nature of foodservice and its way of working are different from the retail sector. And we'll assume that you consider these differences too great to be overcome. But nevertheless, you can see that foodservice offers benefits to you – perhaps it's top line growth, or perhaps it's incremental profits, or maybe it's the chance to get closer to the people who actually consume your product. So, you feel you just can't give up.

My one piece of advice is that if you decide to get into supplying the foodservice sector, you should build a Chinese Wall between your foodservice business and your retail supply business. That means you should reduce to the minimum contact between the two parts of your business (obviously sharing the 'sector neutral' activities like bookkeeping and human resources). You should consider building this wall as high as you can within your organisation, perhaps right up to the legal status of your company – create a new business with a new structure covering management, production, financing. And if that's too drastic, have someone (or more) on your board who has a clear and loud voice for foodservice. You should consider a separate P&L, and production capabilities so that they don't have to continually play off the differing requirements of your large retail customers against the bespoke and much smaller needs of your foodservice customers.

Too often I have seen combined salesforces trying to meet the needs of foodservice and struggling for resources against the more compelling needs of retail. The strains build and become unacceptable. You should definitely split out sales – have separate foodservice and retail salesforces right up to separate responsibilities at board level.

These are just some ways that you can build your Chinese Wall. The stronger and higher it is, the better.

But you must allow for some information and new ideas to permeate the wall – ideas about developing new products for example or having market or trade promotions that make sense for both foodservice and retail markets simultaneously.

And my other suggestion is to outsource your foodservice activities to a business that understands that business. There are options here to consider. You can use a sales agency that focuses on the foodservice sector. You can enter into a joint venture with a business that has a sensible fit with products, production, management resources, and skills. You may want to licence your brand to another party. And also consider the concept of 'harmony' – make sure your values are aligned as well as the harder issues too.

These are some of the several ways to approach the conundrum that this book discusses: how to balance the difficulties your business faces in selling to foodservice against the obvious benefits that you have identified in moving forward in the sector.

I have looked at foodservice and I just don't see how I can make it work for my company. What can I do? Consider three options: 1. Decide to ignore foodservice 2. Get on in foodservice by building a Chinese Wall 3. Outsource your foodservice business

And while you are lingering over your coffee...

We're getting to the end, and you have the opportunity to relax for a while and cogitate on the experience. What's it like?

For starters: I've tried to tell it like it is – good and bad points, but without tearing anything apart – or covering anything with a layer of schmaltz (the language of foodservice is taken from around the world – and this word for oily / greasy – is from Poland, via Yiddish).

I have aimed at giving you the benefit of my experience on these matters – experience that I have gained over the past thirty or more years working in the foodservice sector with manufacturers, distributors, operators and investors.

As I said at the start, this book is for you if you are thinking about a future in supplying foodservice – and now your decision will be based on considerations that are different from those that apply to the retail market.

Why do the variations between the foodservice sector and retailing matter? Foodservice is about relations – it's embedded within the world of hospitality. Retailing on the other hand is all about process and efficiency. That means the characteristics which make a person successful in foodservice will not be the same as – and may often be at odds with – those characteristics that make a person do well in retail.

Where personality is concerned, the major distinction involves people skills, the ability to easily form good interpersonal relationships. Of course, getting on with other people, empathy, the ability to inspire and motivate are all important for anyone whether leader or led, in both foodservice and retailing.

But the relative importance of these characteristics is different in the two markets. The successful foodservice person gets on well with people, is probably gregarious or at least willing to talk, is not particularly turned on by technology, is happy to spend an hour or two in someone else's company (or networking) for its own sake.

That's not to say that this person isn't conscious of the bottom line, doesn't know how to move the business forward, isn't adept at encouraging efficiencies in the kitchen, and so on. It's just that these things are lower down the list of priorities for foodservice success. That is because the business of foodservice is all about being friendly and welcoming.

This element of hospitality extends not only to the restaurant or pub, but also to the day-to-day workplace, whether it's a staff canteen or school kitchen, care home or hospital. It affects everyone whom the foodservice person encounters. Clearly, and very significantly, this includes the customer, but it also includes suppliers whether they supply food or drink, provide premises or accountancy services, service kitchen equipment or clean the floors.

All of these people, and many more, are touched, if that's not too strong a word, by the hospitality bug. And they react accordingly to their own kind – they become more hospitable. It's people who themselves share the hospitality bug who are successful suppliers to the food-service sector.

And the more the successful ones have the hospitality gene, the more successful they are likely to be in working in or supplying the sector. People who don't have the right attributes for success in foodservice get winnowed out.

The successful supplier to the foodservice sector – whether it's a corporate entity like a delivered wholesaler or an individual such as a national account manager – does not have the same balance of priorities, the same genes, as the wholesaler that successfully supplies the retail sector or successfully handles the Tesco account.

So here is a rule: the successful retail salesman is not the same as the successful foodservice salesman.

Many businesses do not recognise this, and the results are unfortunate. The successful foodservice salesman is seen as inferior to the successful retail salesman – with no justification. People with the hospitality gene to the fore are entrepreneurial, unstructured, driven by people and not things.

What does this mean? It means that foodservice people, and therefore the foodservice world, is characterised by several things. For example, it lags behind in technology – it is a late developer. Why use an electric mixer when you can use a whisk? Why use a computer when it gets in the way of dealing with people?

And decision making can appear chaotic and unstructured. Many foodservice operators, including most successful large companies, make decisions on the fly – I know, I have been selling information to them for years. For example, when evaluating a site for a new restaurant, the foodservice person will decide on the basis of feeling, thinking, but not necessarily knowing.

In addition to the hospitality gene, the foodservice sector possesses several other characteristics that are difficult for retail oriented companies to grasp.

The first is that statistical information is not part of their DNA. Foodservice is able to get by without it and in some sense distrusts it – and accordingly this industry does not constantly collect, analyse, and interpret information in the 21st century manner.

In the retail market, information piles up by the second; terabytes of data are available for analysis and interpretation. Spreadsheets and PowerPoint presentations proliferate. A whole world of jargon exists to interpret and then communicate what it all means. Category management becomes a science, and woe betide you if you don't understand it

So, in foodservice, this kind of information that suppliers expect to see is often lacking. The data valued here is very different – what counts is what you know and how you relate to what the other person knows.

Now, I shouldn't go too far here, because data is used in the foodservice industry even though those who use it are in a minority. And there are some areas where data is important. For example, category management in the supply chain is used to market products successfully to the foodservice sector. And category management relies on data. Successful fast-food chains grow business by opening outlets in places where customer traffic – the type and number of customers in the right need state and with willingness to spend – will support their business model. Their decisions rely on acquiring information about customers and locations so that the two can be matched.

A second characteristic of foodservice that retail finds difficult to deal with is that foodservice presents a smaller market opportunity than retail for most products; secondly, bespoke (or short-run) products are much more likely to be found here. At the same time, there are many more buying points in foodservice than in retail. The result therefore is that developing the foodservice market is a slow burn process, in which word of mouth and past experience are much more important parts of the marketing mix than in retail

So now we have come full circle and are back on page one. You have reached the point where you need to decide what to do about the foodservice sector. I am not suggesting that I have provided every last thought on the foodservice sector – and I hope you don't take everything you have read here as the final word. There are, no doubt, many other factors you must take into account. For example, you may already have a number of foodservice accounts as customers. Perhaps you are doing some business with a pub group, and you also have a great and growing relationship with a restaurant chain. But individually and together they don't amount to a new business strategy – consequently you feel the need to tidy up the sector and decide how you will achieve scale

Or perhaps you have a new plant – or storage facility – that is about to come on stream, and you need additional business to fill it and cover its overheads. You believe that foodservice, which for you may be an unexploited sector, would perhaps provide the additional volume you require.

Or maybe your shareholders are pushing you for growth, and you can't see sufficient of it forthcoming – in a profitable manner at least – from the retail sector.

These are but a few examples of the many reasons that I've heard over the years from management as to why it decided to get into foodservice. And you will have to take these factors into account when deciding what to do about foodservice and, assuming that you see foodservice as a viable opportunity, how you should think about optimising the factors for your success.

But first—ask youself some questions. Do I seriously want to devote energies and resources to tackling this sector?

The next question is: What plans do I have for the sector – in terms of quantum (how much, how profitable) and the timing (this year, next year, in five years)?

And finally, What does my plan look like – what sectors, what products, what resources, and above all what expectations and how realistic are they?

Without asking and answering these questions you may stand in danger of making the incorrect strategic decisions – and the wrong tactical ones too. You will need to understand foodservice through and through, especially in its significant differences from retail, as an antidote to its complexity.

In those businesses with a corporate focus on selling to the retail sector, too often plans for the foodservice sector are built with a retail mindset (and we have seen how dangerous that can be), and then are executed for the foodservice sector without sufficient detailed knowledge of this complex sector. And too often as well, not enough time is built into the plan to allow for all the uncertainty that is inherent in foodservice, that adds to manufacturing costs, and slows down foodservice decision making. Not enough leeway on time, or insufficient provision for extra costs, are built into the budget. Timescales are unrealistic and investment is inadequate.

When that happens, pretty soon plans unravel or, at least forecasts and hoped-for sales don't emerge, or if they do they are encouraged to do so at profitability levels well below expectations.

So, lower than expected sales or less than hoped for profitability, possibly coupled with a string of broken promises about the timing of an upturn in fortunes, means that the corporate switch gets turned off. And the foodservice sector which not long ago was going to be the route to riches is now so broken that it affects the corporate KPIs (gross margins, EBITDA, cash flow and that sort of thing). The decision then is taken to get out of foodservice.

And all because not enough attention was paid to getting under the skin of foodservice. Not enough time was allowed for gaining the necessary understanding to make the right decisions and manage corporate expectations for timing and profitability, as well as sales.

So, the moral, is clear. Make sure you understand the foodservice sector in all its frustrating complexity and its high promise too.

Finally – I have seen many companies go through the cycle of exciting planning, committed roll out, then unfulfilled expectations, and the final decision to pull out of foodservice. I have seen the self-same companies start all over again after three years when the current management crop has moved on and a new cohort has arrived with a mission to grow the company through opening up foodservice. And so the cycle gets repeated – and re-repeated – and re-re-repeated. To make sure you do not find yourself in this situation, before you commit to plans, make sure you understand foodservice properly.

In getting down to the how to construct these plans, you might also find the following summary of all the key points that I've included in this book helpful. Out of my catalogue of about 500 slides that I use in various forums to explain and analyse the foodservice sector for people just like you, people tell me that this summation is the most useful of all – I hope you agree:

Twelve reasons why retail is different to foodservice:

	Retail	Foodservice
1.	Impersonal	Hospitable
2.	Consumers buy brands	Operators buy from companies
3.	Quantum leaps	Small steps
4.	Short-term results	Long-haul outlook
5.	Systems driven	Entrepreneurial
6.	Big turnover	Smaller turnover
7.	Few buying points	Many buying points
8.	Mass market	Bespoke market
9.	Media focus	Trade focus
10.	Simple supply chain	Distributors involved in supply chain
11.	Long production runs	Short production runs
12.	**Senior management have experience**	**Senior management have expectations**

Lightning Source UK Ltd.
Milton Keynes UK
UKHW021024281118
333119UK00003B/130/P